cook's guide to
poultry
& game

cook's guide to
poultry & game

LUCY KNOX AND KEITH RICHMOND

southwater

This edition is published by Southwater, an imprint of Anness Publishing Ltd, Hermes House,
88–89 Blackfriars Road, London SE1 8HA; tel. 020 7401 2077; fax 020 7633 9499

www.southwaterbooks.com; www.annesspublishing.com

If you like the images in this book and would like to investigate using them for publishing, promotions or advertising,
please visit our website www.practicalpictures.com for more information.

UK agent: The Manning Partnership Ltd; tel. 01225 478444; fax 01225 478440; sales@manning-partnership.co.uk
UK distributor: Grantham Book Services Ltd; tel. 01476 541080; fax 01476 541061; orders@gbs.tbs-ltd.co.uk
North American agent/distributor: National Book Network; tel. 301 459 3366; fax 301 429 5746; www.nbnbooks.com
Australian agent/distributor: Pan Macmillan Australia; tel. 1300 135 113; fax 1300 135 103; customer.service@macmillan.com.au
New Zealand agent/distributor: David Bateman Ltd; tel. (09) 415 7664; fax (09) 415 8892

Publisher: Joanna Lorenz
Managing Editor: Linda Fraser
Senior Editor: Margaret Malone
Designer: Nigel Partridge
Photographers: Craig Robertson (recipe section) and Janine Hosegood (reference)
Stylist: Helen Trent
Food for Photography: Joanna Farrow and Bridget Sargeson, assisted by
Victoria Walters (recipe section); and Annabel Ford (reference section)
Editorial Reader: Joy Wotton

© Anness Publishing Limited 2001, 2008

A CIP catalogue record for this book is available from the British Library.

Previously published as part of a larger compendium, *The World Encyclopedia of Meat, Game and Poultry*

ETHICAL TRADING POLICY
Because of our ongoing ecological investment programme, you, as our customer, can
have the pleasure and reassurance of knowing that a tree is being cultivated on your
behalf to naturally replace the materials used to make the book you are holding. For
further information about this scheme, go to www.annesspublishing.com/trees

NOTES

Bracketed terms are intended for American readers. Medium (US large) eggs are used unless otherwise stated. For all
recipes, quantities are given in both metric and imperial measures and, where appropriate, measures are also given in
standard cups and spoons. Follow one set, but not a mixture, because they are not interchangeable. Standard spoon and
cup measures are level. 1 tsp = 5ml, 1 tbsp = 15ml, 1 cup = 250ml/8fl oz. Australian standard tablespoons are 20ml.
Australian readers should use 3 tsp in place of 1 tbsp for measuring small quantities of gelatine, flour, salt etc.

CONTENTS

INTRODUCTION

Poultry and game have always been popular meats and in many countries they are the food for a celebration, a feast or any special occasion. More than just festive foods, however, poultry and game are enormously versatile, and can be enjoyed whole, or cut and prepared in many ways. They can be fried, grilled (broiled), poached or stewed, served with pasta, rice, grains or vegetables or cooked with just about anything.

Such versatility is also evident in the exciting range of new meats available – such as alligator, wild boar and buffalo – whose flavours and textures bring new interest to everyday cooking.

Wild and domesticated birds and animals

Meat has been eaten for as long as man has been able to catch the animals. At first the animals were wild, but it wasn't long before ancient man began to successfully domesticate animals such as chickens, geese and ducks, among others, for their flesh and for their eggs.

Below: Free-range chickens have plenty of room to wander about – a far cry from the tiny cages in which intensively reared hens are cooped.

While most of the meat eaten today is from domesticated and farm-reared birds and animals not all is – such wild meat is known as game. Our ancestors ate far more game than is consumed nowadays, and some once popular birds, such as swans and peacocks, have so diminished in number that they are no longer eaten, while other birds and animals, such as quail and wild boar, are now reared for the table in farms. Nowadays, most game is protected by strict laws and can be killed only at certain times of the year.

Factors influencing choice

Until very recently meat was far and away the most expensive component of a meal and, in times of shortages, it was inevitably the first ingredient on which to cut back. Throughout history people have made the most of meat by serving it with economical starchy ingredients and accompaniments such as pastry, dumplings or Yorkshire puddings to eke it out.

In fact, it is thanks entirely to the less affluent members of society that we have so many different recipes for cooking meat. Stews, casseroles,

Above: Geese have long been domesticated, but they remain a seasonal treat as efforts to rear them intensively are unsuccessful.

tagines, hot-pots, pies and cassoulets are among the hundreds of ways devised by ordinary people for using the poorer, less tender cuts of meat.

It is not only cost that determines how much, or which, meat is eaten. Consumption also varies according to religion, custom and taste. In those communities that observe Judaism, for example, there are numerous food laws. Only animals that chew the cud and have cloven hooves can be eaten. All others, including rabbit, horses and pigs, are considered unclean and are forbidden. All meat must be koshered before it is eaten, which means that it must be slaughtered by cutting the animal's throat to let the blood drain. For this reason, game that has been hunted and shot is also not allowed.

Improvements in quality

In most countries, however, there are no religious laws underpinning meat preparation, and consequently the meat available in shops continues to change, as methods of breeding and butchery improve. Meat today is vastly superior in flavour and texture to that available even 20 years ago. Farmers have responded to concerns about healthy

Above: Kangaroo is hunted in every state in Australia, and the lean, flavourful meat is becoming more widely available in supermarkets and butchers in Europe.

Above: Alligator is popular in the southern states of America. These animals are now reared in farms to protect the wild species from extinction.

Below: Ostriches, whose natural habitats include Australia and Africa, are now reared in farms in Scotland.

eating, and are breeding animals that provide leaner meat. In addition, they are realizing that the more care lavished on poultry or game the better the meat. Customers in turn are demanding this too, both because of concern about the welfare of animals and birds and because of a desire for good, lean meat.

There is no doubt that free-range chicken tastes better than its intensively reared equivalent. As a result, more and more farmers are reverting to traditional, often organic, methods where animals are allowed to graze freely outdoors, raised on a diet free from both chemicals and pesticides.

Organic and traditionally reared poultry is becoming increasingly available from specialist butchers and many supermarkets. It generally costs a little more than meat from intensively reared poultry, but is considered to be superior in every respect, being healthier, more flavoursome, and with a leaner and more tender texture. Most of us are also happier knowing that the meat we are eating comes from an animal that was properly treated when alive, and humanely killed.

New meat varieties

Other meats have also become newly fashionable both in their country of origin and elsewhere. Meats from animals such as alligator, crocodile, emu, kangaroo, ostrich and wild boar can nowadays be bought in butchers' shops and supermarkets almost as easily as poultry and game. These new meats appeal not only because they taste very good but also because they are lean and tender. Like some of the traditional "game" animals and birds, such as deer and quail, many of these animals are no longer hunted in the wild, but are bred for the table in special farms.

Using this book

The first part of this book gives a detailed guide to all the different types of poultry, game and new meats, with useful information on buying, storing and handling, as well as instructions on preparation and cooking.

The recipe section includes classic as well as some modern recipes. You will find something here for every meal, whether it's a romantic meal for two or an impressive roast for a big occasion.

KITCHEN ESSENTIALS

The following section contains all you need to know about selecting and preparing all types of poultry and game birds as well as less familiar types of meat such as ostrich, crocodile and wild boar. These meats are wonderfully versatile, and can be fried, grilled, roasted or stir-fried for fabulous, easy meals.

Being small and easy to keep, chickens have been domesticated for thousands of years. As was the practice with other animals, early chickens were reared not only for food, but they also played their part in Roman sacred rites. Originating from Malaysian jungle birds, the chickens we eat today are directly descended from the fowl that were first domesticated in the Indus valley more than 4,000 years ago. Chicken farming is not a modern industry – even before the Romans turned their attentions to hatching methods, the Egyptians had already done so.

Although the European idea of hens pecking about the farmyard conjures an idyllic image, in many early, poor farms that was not always the case. Chickens were kept in backyards or small gardens as well as on farms. Many birds were sadly undernourished and forced to scavenge in every unhygienic nook and cranny. Their ends were often as undignified as their lives: neck wrung or topped with a blunt chopper, which resulted in them running around in headless circles. So the country cock that made it to the peasant's table was likely to be a sad culinary offering, with little meat and necessitating hours of boiling, rendering minimal flavour to all but the soup.

In the 20th century, when small traditional farms were dotted all over the countryside, chickens were kept for their eggs and killed only when they were past their laying best. Eventually, old cocks were also sent to the pot – for a thorough boiling or stewing. With neat hen houses, spacious pens and often having access to the orchard, the hen's greatest fear was the fox, but a good farmer (or his wife) would guard against that ransacking intruder.

Before the advent of intensive rearing, chicken became a luxury food and a roasting bird was an occasional treat. Intensive rearing brought chicken to every table, not only as a special treat, but also as an everyday staple; however, quantity superseded quality, and flavour and texture diminished. As the conditions in which battery hens are kept have been exposed and the

resulting hygiene and health problems realized, so public outcry has forced a reversal towards traditional methods. Rules and regulations vary and terms are many and confusing.

Ultimately, the better the conditions under which poultry are reared, the better the product they yield. Whether the end concern is the welfare of the poultry or the quality of the meat, the means to both are the same. If you want good-quality chicken, buy those that have been well-reared.

Nutrition

Chicken is rich in high-quality protein, providing all the essential amino acids required by the body for growth and repair. Chicken provides B-group vitamins, especially niacin. It also provides iron (more in the leg meat than the breast meat) as well as the minerals copper and selenium. The white meat

Above: Cockerels aren't often eaten, although castrated birds, known as capons are available in some countries.

is low in fat (the fat is found in and under the skin) and contains a lower proportion of saturated fat than meat.

Choice of bird

Apart from the standard intensively reared chicken, there is a choice of birds raised by different farming methods. These are available as whole birds or in portions.

Free-range birds are not reared in battery conditions. The laws vary according to the country of origin.

Corn-fed chickens are easily recognized by their bright yellow skin, which loses its colour during cooking and yields golden fat, that also diminishes in colour during

cooking. The colour is probably due to the colour in the corn feed.

Organic birds are raised in humane conditions, fed on a natural and (usually) traditional-style diet. They do not have lurid-coloured skin. Standards and conditions relating to the particular scheme or terms by which the birds are classed as organic are usually outlined on the packaging. Organic organizations and authorities readily provide information on their standards.

Below from left: corn-fed, free-range and organic chickens

Buying

Poultry can be bought fresh, chilled or frozen. Look for birds with a clear, soft skin (there should be no blemishes or bruises). A soft, thin skin shows that the bird is young; the tougher the skin, the older the bird. The bigger the bird, the better its value because the proportion of meat to bone will be higher. As well as whole birds, chicken is available in a choice of portions such as quarters, legs, wings, thighs, breast portions and drumsticks. The portions may be on the bone or boneless, with or without skin. Sliced, diced and minced (ground) chicken breast portions are also available. Stir-fry strips, marinated cuts and stuffed portions are all sold fresh or frozen.

Storing

Place poultry that has been purchased loose in a deep dish and cover it closely. Check pre-packed poultry to make sure that the packs are sealed before placing them in the refrigerator. Store in the coldest part of the refrigerator.

Below: Boiling chicken

Use pre-packed poultry by the date suggested or loose poultry within about two days of purchase.

Raw, fresh poultry can be frozen successfully. Remove the giblets from a whole bird, if necessary. Wrap portions individually in clear film (plastic wrap) or freezer film. Pack the poultry or portions in a freezer bag and seal tightly.

The best way to thaw frozen poultry is in the refrigerator. Place in a container, cover closely and leave in the refrigerator overnight. Remove the giblets from a whole bird as soon as possible.

Handling

Poultry is particularly susceptible to bacterial growth, which can cause food poisoning if it is allowed to contaminate uncooked foods that are eaten raw (such as salads) or if the poultry is eaten without being thoroughly cooked.

Always keep poultry chilled, as bacteria thrive in warmth. Select poultry towards the end of a shopping session and avoid leaving it to warm up in the car before going home. Unpack and chill it promptly. Leave the poultry in the refrigerator until you need it.

Before preparing raw poultry, assemble all the equipment and dishes you will need. Weigh out all the other ingredients you are using, then unpack and cut, coat or prepare the poultry. When making an entire meal in one session, including dishes that are to be served uncooked or ready-cooked ingredients, such as cooked seafood or meat in a first course, salads, or desserts, it is a good idea to prepare these foods first before handling the raw poultry to avoid cross-contamination.

Thoroughly wash utensils, surfaces and hands after handling and cooking poultry. Remember to wash utensils used with part-cooked poultry before using them with cooked poultry.

Left: Organic chickens are raised in humane, free-range, conditions.

Below: A capon is a large bird with a high proportion of white meat.

Stewing or boiling chicken

Also known as a boiling hen or fowl, this is an older bird. It requires long, slow simmering as the flesh is tough, but its flavour is excellent. As a guide to age, the older the chicken, the harder and more rigid the breastbone. Boiling fowl are not readily available these days as demand is low, so they have to be sourced from a specialist butcher. Stewing chickens are used for pies, fricassées, ballottines and galantines and, most often of all, in soups, stews and casseroles.

Capon

This is a young cockerel that has been castrated and then fattened on a special diet to make it plump and flavourful. The practice is prohibited in many countries, including Britain. Capons are large birds and can weigh between 2.7–4.5kg/6–10lb. In the past they were often cooked for celebration meals at Christmas and Thanksgiving in place of turkey. They have a fairly large proportion of white meat to dark.

Cook well, eat well

Poultry should be cooked through, without any sign of raw flesh or juices. This is the way to ensure all the bacteria are destroyed. To check if poultry is cooked, pierce the thickest area of the meat with a thin metal skewer. If there is any sign of pink in either the flesh or the juices, then the meat is not cooked and it must be returned to the heat or the oven for further cooking.

TYPES OF SMALL POULTRY

Roasting chicken

Sometimes called a roaster, this is a young cockerel or hen about 12 weeks old. Roasting chickens usually weigh about 1.3kg/3lb, but they may be as big as 3kg/6–7lb. Older birds (up to 20 weeks old) and up to 4.5kg/10lb in weight are available from specialist butchers' shops.

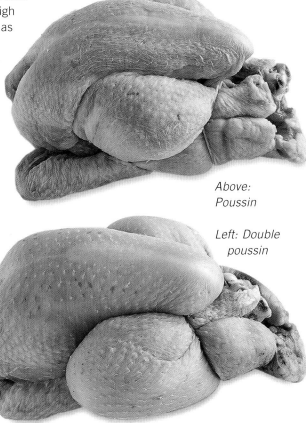

Above: Poussin

Left: Double poussin

Left: Roasting chicken

Poussin

This is the French name for a young chicken, four to six weeks old and weighing 350–675g/12oz–1½lb. Each bird provides an individual portion. Poussins, which are also sometimes called spring chickens, have a tender, delicate flavour. They can be roasted, often with a moist stuffing, and they can also be spatchcocked and grilled (broiled), pan-fried or cooked on a barbecue.

Double poussin

A larger, older poussin that weighs about 900g/2lb and is about six weeks old. Double poussins are big enough to serve two people. Like poussins, they are tender, but they lack flavour.

Above: Chicken portions include the leg quarter, drumsticks and thighs.

Above: Boneless chicken breast portion (top) and a chicken supreme with part of the wingbone.

Rock Cornish hen

This small North American cross-breed was developed from White Rock and Cornish chickens and is sometimes called a Rock Cornish game hen. These small birds are four to six weeks old and can weigh up to 1.2kg/2½lb. The flesh is white and flavourful, though the ratio of bone to meat is high, so each hen will usually serve only one person.

Below: An oven-ready guinea fowl, which has a slightly gamier flavour than chicken.

Guinea fowl

These are domestic fowl, which have been raised in Europe for centuries, but originally came from the coast of Guinea in West Africa. They are tender with slightly dry flesh that resembles pheasant. The flesh is not distinctly game-like in flavour, but it leans more in that direction than towards chicken. Guinea fowl are generally cooked as for chicken or pheasant, but at a high temperature – for example the birds should be barded and roasted in an oven preheated to 230°C/450°F/Gas 8 for 25–30 minutes. Alternatively, the birds can be braised or casseroled.

Cuts of chicken

A wide range of different portions are available, both on and off the bone. **Quarters** include either the leg or the wing joint, the latter having a large portion of breast meat. The leg joint includes the thigh and drumstick. **Other portions** include **thighs**, which are small, neat joints, **drumsticks**, which take a surprisingly long time to cook as the meat is quite compact, and **wings**, which have very little meat. **Breast portions** are sold on or off the bone, skinned or unskinned; these portions include only the white meat. Cuts include **boneless breasts**, which may be sold as fillets, **supremes**, which include the wingbone and **part-boned breasts**, which still have the short piece of bone leading into the wing and the breastbone.

PREPARING SMALL POULTRY

These techniques are suitable for chicken as well as other poultry, such as guinea fowl and poussin, and game birds, such as pheasant.

Jointing a bird

Many recipes specify particular joints of poultry or game and, although you can buy them ready-prepared, with the right equipment it is actually quite straightforward to joint a bird at home.

There are various joints into which the bird can be cut, depending on the recipe. For example, it can be cut into four or eight pieces. Use a large, sharp knife and poultry shears for cutting through meat and bone. The following gives four small portions from each side of the bird, eight pieces in total – two wings, two breasts, two drumsticks and two thighs.

1 Put the bird breast-side up on a chopping board. Use a sharp knife to remove the leg by cutting through the skin and then through the thigh joint. Repeat with the leg on the other side.

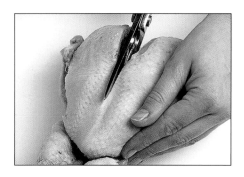

2 Following the line of the breastbone and using poultry shears, cut the breast neatly in half, making the cut as clean as possible.

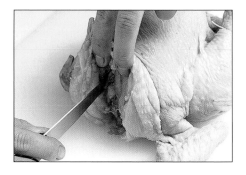

3 Turn the bird over and cut out the backbone. Leave the wings attached.

4 Cut each breast in half, leaving a portion of the breast attached to the wing.

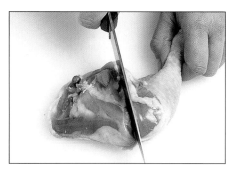

5 Cut each leg through the knee joint to separate the thigh and drumstick.

6 Using poultry shears, cut off the wing tip at the first joint.

Preparing a bird for roasting

Very little preparation is needed to roast a bird, but the following techniques make life easier.

Removing the wishbone

The wishbone is the arched bone at the neck end of the bird. It does not have to be removed, but the breast can be carved more easily without it.

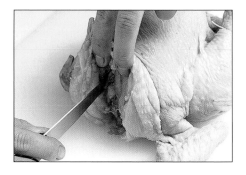

1 Using a small, sharp knife gently pull back the skin from the neck cavity and carefully cut around the wishbone.

2 Gently scrape away the meat from the wishbone, then cut it away at the base and pull it out.

> ### Make a lucky wish
> When the roast bird is served, it is traditional for two people to pull the wishbone until it snaps. Each person is allowed to use only the little finger to hold the end of one side of the bone. On the signal to pull, the person who ends up with the larger arched top of the bone is entitled to make a wish. So, remove the wishbone and someone will be deprived of a lucky wish!

Trussing with skewers

This is a quick and useful method for a larger bird that has a greater quantity of meat and is therefore more rigid, so firmer in shape.

1 Push one metal skewer through both sections of the wing, into the skin of the neck and straight out through the wing on the other side.

2 Push in the second metal skewer firmly, pressing it straight through the thighs and the tail cavity.

Trussing with string

Tying a bird with string keeps it in a neat, compact shape during roasting and helps it to cook more evenly.

1 Season the bird and tuck the wing tips and neck flap underneath.

2 Tie a piece of string around the legs and under the flap of skin.

3 Bring the string towards the neck end, passing it between the legs.

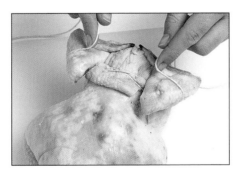

4 Turn the bird over and wrap the string around the wings to keep them flat.

5 Pull the string tight to bring the wings together, and tie neatly.

Spatchcocking a bird

This is a method of splitting and then flattening a whole bird so that it can be grilled (broiled) or roasted quickly.

1 Tuck the wings under the bird and remove the wishbone. Turn the bird over and use a pair of poultry shears to split it along each side of the backbone. Remove the backbone.

2 Turn the bird over, and place on a chopping board breast-side uppermost. Then press down firmly with the heel of one hand on the middle of the breast to flatten the bird against the board.

3 To keep the bird flat, push a metal skewer through the wings and breast. Then push a second metal skewer parallel to the first, through the thighs and the tip of the breast.

Tunnel boning a bird

This is a method of part-boning a bird from the breast to the joints. The skin is left in one piece and the bird is ready to stuff. This is easy with a larger bird, but can be fiddly and difficult to manage with small birds.

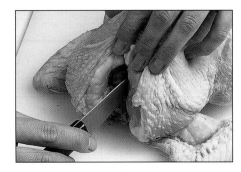

1 Pull back the skin around the neck of the bird, then carefully cut out and remove the wishbone.

2 Feel inside the cavity for the wing joint, then use a small, sharp knife to cut the bones free as you separate the breastbone from the meat and skin from one side of the bird.

3 Find the curved bone and carefully pull it out. Continue cutting away the meat from the bone until you reach the wing joint.

4 Cut through the wing joint firmly using the tip of the knife, then repeat on the other side of the bird. Pull the meat back from the carcass and continue cutting the flesh from the bone, keeping the knife as near to the bone as possible. Turn the carcass from one side to another, and work towards the tail end of the bird. Sever the leg joints when you reach them, leaving the bones attached to the leg meat.

5 Carefully cut and ease the skin away from the breastbone, then turn the bird outside in so that the skin is now on the outside. The finished bird retains the joints, but the central part of the body is completely boneless.

Preparing boneless breast fillets

The advantage of preparing fillets yourself is that the rest of the carcass can be jointed and used to make a well-flavoured stock.

1 Joint the bird into portions, but keep the breasts whole.

2 Use your fingers to pull the skin and thin membrane away from the breast. Use a small, sharp knife to carefully cut the meat off the rib bone and any remaining breastbone.

3 Remove the thin, white central tendons from the breast, using a small, sharp knife.

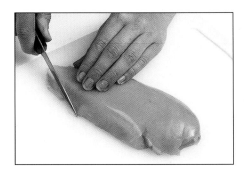

4 Trim away any pieces of fat and untidy edges from the breast portion.

Preparing escalopes

A chicken breast portion yields two escalopes (US scallop). The technique below can be used with other poultry – duck and turkey breast portions can be sliced into several escalopes, depending on the size of the breast.

1 Place the skinless, boneless breast portion flat on a chopping board and, using a large, sharp knife, slice the breast in half horizontally. To cut a thin, even slice, hold your hand flat on top of the chicken breast portion as you cut, to prevent it from moving.

2 Lay in turn each slice of chicken between sheets of baking parchment and beat out gently and evenly until the chicken is thin and flat, using a meat mallet or rolling pin.

Cutting strips for stir-frying

Tender poultry is ideal for stir-frying. Use a flattened escalope for stir-fry strips (see above).

Lay the thin escalope on a board and cut it across into fine strips. When cut across the grain in this way, the meat cooks extremely quickly.

Skinning and boning chicken thighs

When boned, chicken thighs yield a neat nugget of well-flavoured meat.

1 Use a sharp knife to loosen the skin, then pull it away from the meat.

2 Carefully cut the flesh lengthways along the main thigh bone, then cut the bone out, trimming the meat close to the bone, and then lift the bone away. Continue cutting out the bones, leaving the meat open and flat.

Making kebabs

The thigh meat is ideal for kebabs. First skin and bone the thigh (as above).

1 Cut the thigh meat across the grain into about four pieces, using a small, sharp knife.

2 Fold slightly elongated pieces of meat in half and thread them on to skewers. Add pieces of vegetable between the meat – try button (white) mushrooms and chunks of red and green (bell) pepper – they complement chicken and will cook in the same time.

Chicken Kiev

Deep-fried chicken breast portions filled with garlic butter is a Russian invention popular world-wide.

SERVES FOUR

INGREDIENTS
115g/4oz/½ cup butter, softened
2 garlic cloves, crushed
finely grated rind of 1 lemon
30ml/2 tbsp chopped fresh tarragon
4 skinless chicken breast fillets (with wing bone attached)
1 egg, lightly beaten
115g/4oz/2 cups fresh breadcrumbs
oil, for deep frying
salt and ground black pepper

1 Beat together the butter, garlic, lemon rind and tarragon with salt and pepper and shape into a 5cm/2in long rectangular block. Wrap in clear film (plastic wrap). Chill for 1 hour.

2 Beat out the chicken supremes gently until fairly thin. Cut the butter lengthways into four pieces and put one in the centre of each chicken supreme. Fold the edges over the butter and secure with cocktail sticks (toothpicks).

3 Place the beaten egg and breadcrumbs in separate shallow dishes. Dip the chicken pieces first in beaten egg and then in breadcrumbs to coat evenly. Dip them a second time in each. Chill for at least 1 hour.

4 Heat the oil in a large pan to 180°C/350°F. Deep fry the chicken for 6–8 minutes, or until the chicken is cooked and the coating golden. Drain on kitchen paper. Remove the cocktail sticks from the chicken and serve hot.

COOKING SMALL POULTRY

Tender birds can be poached, roasted, grilled (broiled), cooked on a barbecue, griddled or fried in a shallow pan or, once coated in breadcumbs or batter, in deep oil. Since older, tough birds are rarely available nowadays, tender poultry are also used in slow-cooked casseroles and stews. If you do have an older bird, it should be cooked by long, gentle and moist methods, such as braising or stewing.

Roasting

Small poultry birds, such as chickens, poussins and guinea fowl, are easy to roast. When cooking a slightly larger bird, requiring longer cooking, you may need to cover the top of the breast loosely with foil when it is a light golden brown. Remove the foil for the final 15 minutes cooking time to complete the browning.

1 Rub the breast and the top of the bird generously with butter. If you are stuffing the bird, stuff it at the neck end only before trussing and then tuck the neck skin under.

2 Place the bird breast-side down in the roasting pan for the first 30 minutes of the cooking time.

3 Turn and baste the bird, then continue cooking for the calculated time. Remove the pan from the oven and baste the bird every 15 minutes.

4 When the bird is completely cooked (see tip on checking cooking progess, opposite), remove the roasting pan from the oven and then cover the cooked bird tightly with foil. Leave it to rest in a warm place for 10–15 minutes before carving and serving. Either do this in the roasting pan or, if you wish to make gravy or a sauce with the pan juices and fat, then transfer the bird to a warmed serving platter or carving dish.

Roasting times for small poultry
Preheat the oven to 200°C/400°F/
Gas 6, or 230°C/450°F/Gas 8 for guinea fowl. Calculate the cooking time according to the weight of the bird. Weigh the bird when it has been trimmed and with any stuffing added.
Chicken allow 20 minutes per 450g/
1lb, plus an extra 20 minutes.
Poussin allow 50–60 minutes total roasting time.
Guinea fowl allow 15 minutes per 450g/1lb, plus 15 minutes.

Grilling

This is a quick cooking method for smaller birds and portions. For even, thorough cooking, split a whole bird in half or spatchcock it. The birds can be flavoured with garlic, herbs or lemon rind. Rub flavouring ingredients into the bird 1–2 hours in advance to allow the flavours to infuse.

1 Preheat the grill (broiler) on the hottest setting. Brush the bird or birds with oil and season well.

2 Place skin-side up on a rack in a grill pan and cook well below the heat source so the meat has time to cook through before the skin overbrowns.

3 Allow about 40 minutes cooking for poussin, turning them frequently and brushing with oil to keep them moist.

Griddling boneless breast fillets

This is a healthy way of cooking, allowing fat to drain away between the ridges of the pan and preventing the meat from becoming greasy.

1 Brush the breast fillets with a little vegetable oil.

2 Preheat the griddle until it is almost smoking, then lay the breast fillets on it – don't overload the pan, or the meat will begin to steam rather than brown.

3 Cook until the meat is well browned underneath, and firm and white inside. Turn the fillets over using a pair of tongs or a spatula.

4 Continue cooking the chicken until the second side is well browned and the meat is firm and white throughout.

Barbecuing portions

Poultry must be cooked through, so it is important to ensure that the barbecue is properly heated and fuelled with enough charcoal to burn hot enough and long enough to cook the poultry thoroughly. Position the grilling rack well away from the hot coals so that the meat has plenty of time to cook through before the skin is overcooked.

1 Cut deep slashes into thick portions that require lengthy cooking. This will ensure that they cook through as well as giving the cooked poultry a good flavour. Make two or three cuts across larger drumsticks or poultry quarters. There is no need to slash small drumsticks or tender breast meat.

2 Marinating flavours poultry before cooking and provides a good basting mixture to keep it moist during cooking. Olive oil, chopped garlic, chopped fresh herbs and chopped fresh red or green chillies bring full flavours to chicken. Mix together the ingredients in a deep, non-metal container.

3 Add the poultry to the marinade and turn the pieces to coat them thoroughly. Cover and chill for at least 30 minutes or for up to 24 hours.

4 To cook, place the poultry portions on the grill rack, brush with marinade and cook over the hot coals. Turn the pieces frequently to ensure that the portions cook evenly, brushing with more of the marinade to keep the meat moist.

Careful cooking

Barbecues Large drumsticks and thick, dense chicken portions, such as whole leg quarters taste excellent when cooked on a barbecue, but they do require attention to ensure that they are cooked through. One solution is to poach the portions in just enough stock to cover until they are only just cooked – this will take about 20–30 minutes. Leave to cool in the stock, then transfer to the marinade and chill overnight. Slash the meat and cook as above, until thoroughly reheated and well browned – the result is succulent and delicious meat.

Checking cooking progress When you are cooking on a barbecue or by another method, it is important to test that chicken and other poultry is well cooked before serving. Pierce the thickest area of meat with the point of a small, sharp knife. Check the juices – if there is any sign of pink the meat is not cooked. Then check the meat at the base of the cut, when cooked it will be firm and look white, if it is pink and soft, the bird is not cooked. Use this test on portions and whole birds. On a whole bird, the area behind the thigh takes longest to cook.

Pan-frying

The important point to remember when frying poultry is that it must be cooked through. Escalopes (US scallops) and boneless breast portions cook quickly, so they are ideal for speedy pan-frying over a high heat. Breast meat on the bone takes longer and requires closer attention to ensure it is evenly cooked through. Uneven, thicker portions, particularly denser thigh and leg meat on the bone, require careful cooking and turning. With larger pieces, reduce the heat to low once the chicken is browned and cook it very slowly to prevent over-browning.

1 Heat a little olive oil in a large, non-stick frying pan.

2 Add the joints or pieces to the hot oil in the frying pan and cook until they are lightly browned underneath.

3 Turn the joints and cook until they are lightly browned on the second side. Reduce the heat to prevent the joints from becoming too brown before they are cooked through, and continue cooking gently until the meat is cooked. Boneless thighs take about 15–20 minutes. Drumsticks take 30 minutes or longer, depending on their size.

Stir-frying

Poultry will cook very quickly if cut into fine strips. Being very lean, light and tender, chicken and turkey can also be cut into other shapes for stir-frying. Try diced or thinly sliced pieces.

1 Cut lean pieces of breast crossways into thin, even-size strips using a large sharp knife.

2 Heat the empty wok or a large, heavy frying pan until hot before adding a little oil to the wok or pan. Heat the oil until it is very hot.

3 Add the strips of poultry (you may need to do this in batches) and stir-fry using a wooden spatula over a high heat for 3–5 minutes, until browned. The cooking time depends on the quantities, the oil and the type of pan.

Casseroling

Moist cooking methods bring out the flavour of the poultry and offer the opportunity for allowing herbs, spices and aromatics to infuse the light meat thoroughly. Whole birds and joints can be casseroled.

1 Brown the poultry pieces or bird all over first. Remove from the pan before softening chopped onion, carrot, celery and other flavouring ingredients in the fat remaining in the pan.

2 Replace the poultry before adding the chosen liquid – stock, wine, canned tomatoes or even water. Season the casserole well, then bring it just to simmering point. Cover it closely and allow it to simmer very gently on the hob (stovetop). Alternatively, cook in the oven at 180°C/350°F/Gas 4.

> **Cooking times for casseroling**
> **For a whole bird**, allow 20 minutes per 450g/1lb, plus 20 minutes.
> **Large portions** 45–60 minutes.
> **Boneless breast portions** take about 30 minutes.
> **Chunks or diced poultry** 20–40 minutes, depending on their size.

Flavouring and serving poached small poultry

Water is the essential base, providing a good stock. Dry white wine or (hard) cider may be used as part of the liquid – about half and half with water. Dry sherry or vermouth can be added in small quantities to intensify the flavour.

Herbs, such as tarragon or thyme are a good choice, in combination with bay leaves and parsley. Use them in the cooking liquid and add them, freshly chopped, to a plain cream sauce for serving with poached poultry.

As well as lemon, lime or orange go well with poultry. Add the pared rind to the cooking liquid or the grated rind to a plain cream sauce for serving with hot poultry. Flavour mayonnaise or crème fraîche with citrus rind and herbs to complement cold poultry.

Carrots and onions are essential flavouring ingredients; leeks, fennel, and turnips can also be added. For a simple, traditional meal, keep the poached bird hot under tented foil in a warm place, while simmering neat chunks of potato and celeriac in the cooking liquid for 15 minutes, until just tender. Add broccoli florets and green beans about 5 minutes before the end of cooking. Serve the vegetables and seasoned broth with the poultry.

Poaching whole poultry

This is a gentle method for emphasizing the delicate flavour of a bird. The cooked bird can be served hot with a light cream sauce, or allowed to cool in its cooking liquid. The bird can then be jointed, or the meat can be carved from the bones. The meat from poached chicken is moist and succulent, and ideal for using in salads or other cold dishes. To cook a whole bird you will need a large pan or flameproof casserole to hold the bird, flavouring ingredients and plenty of cooking liquid.

1 Truss the whole bird neatly and tightly with string and then place it in a large, heavy pan, stockpot or flameproof casserole dish.

2 Pour in enough liquid (see flavouring and serving poached small poultry, left) to come just to the top of the bird. Heat gently until the liquid is just starting to simmer. Using a large spoon, carefully skim off any scum that rises to the surface of the liquid during the first few minutes of cooking, before adding any flavouring ingredients, spices or herbs.

3 Add the chosen flavouring ingredients to the pan or casserole. A selection of any of the following work well: sliced onions, thick sticks of carrot, a bouquet garni, a strip of pared lemon rind, about 6 black peppercorns and a good sprinkling of salt.

4 Bring the liquid back to simmering point, reduce the heat if necessary and then cover the pan tightly. Cook gently for the calculated time.

5 Use a large draining spoon to lift the bird from the cooking liquid. Transfer the bird to a large dish and use poultry shears and a sharp knife to cut it into serving portions or use as required.

Wines to serve with small poultry

Most young red Burgundies and Beaujolais or, if you prefer white, the distinctively dry steely acidity of Chablis, go well with light poultry dishes like chicken, poussin and guinea fowl. Vouvray from the Loire Valley or a crisp Pinot Gris from Alsace also complement chicken dishes, particularly light, zesty salads.

Straightforward roast guinea fowl will take a medium red – a good red Burgundy – but if the bird has been cooked in a casserole, especially with red wine, go for something fruitier with a more intense flavour, such as a Spanish Rioja or a Shiraz from California, New Zealand or Australia.

When cooking, remember the golden rule: never cook with a wine that you would not be happy to drink. It is a false economy to cook with really cheap wine as it will only spoil good-quality poultry (or meat). And, don't put it all in the pot; it makes sense to serve the same wine to drink that you used for cooking the bird.

TURKEY

The turkey originates from America and was first domesticated by the Aztecs in Mexico. Turkeys were introduced to Europe by the Spanish, and they soon became a popular choice in France, Italy and Britain too.

When early settlers from Britain, France and Holland crossed the Atlantic to North America, the vast flocks of turkey that roamed wild provided them with sustenance. As the first crops failed in land that had not been properly cleared for cultivation, the majority of these first settlers succumbed to starvation and disease.

The plight of the early colonists was not warning enough for the Pilgrim Fathers who landed at Cape Cod in Massachusetts in 1620, after a 66-day voyage from Plymouth, England on the *Mayflower*. Being neither farmers nor trappers, they did not recognize the difficulties they faced. The Pilgrims made it through the winter with the help of the native population who already understood some English from earlier encounters with adventurers. The Native Americans shared their stores of berries, nuts and maize to supplement the settlers' diet of turkey.

In November 1621, on the first anniversary of their arrival, the Pilgrims entertained the Native Americans to a feast to show their appreciation; the

Left: Bronze turkeys like this have a wonderful flavour.

celebration was said to have lasted for three days. This was how the turkey came to be established as the traditional bird for Thanksgiving celebrations and other festive occasions.

Well before turkey became popular in Europe, the bustard and peacock were served, as well as the goose and smaller fowl. Unlike unfamiliar vegetables that were brought from the Americas to Europe and treated with suspicion and caution, Europeans recognized the notion of cooking and eating large birds, so turkey soon became part of affluent feasts. In England, the birds were raised in Norfolk and Suffolk, then herded on

foot into London. Gradually the turkey usurped the goose to become a popular, if expensive, Christmas treat.

Inevitably, its popularity led to the bird being farmed more intensively. Contemporary breeding and rearing have created birds with a larger proportion of breast meat, but much of the meat available is lacking in flavour. The status of the turkey as a bird reserved for feasts has diminished and it is now an everyday choice.

Nutrition

Turkey is a lean source of high-quality protein. It provides B-group vitamins, particularly niacin, and is a good source of zinc, phosphorus, potassium and magnesium. It is also a source of iron.

Buying

Turkeys are available fresh, chilled or frozen. When buying a whole bird, look for a plump, well-rounded breast and legs, and clear, soft and evenly coloured skin. Avoid birds that are bruised, with blemishes or torn skin. Although there are likely to be small cavities left from plucking (particularly on dark-feathered birds), there should not be any patches of feathers. The bird should smell fresh. Turkeys vary enormously in weight, from about 2.75kg/6lb to over 11.25kg/25lb. They can grow up to vast sizes, such as 18kg/40lb, but the average weights available are 4.5–6.3kg/10–14lb.

Left: The best turkeys are free-range, organic birds from a known farm.

Above: A Norfolk Black, which has a very plump breast and a full flavour.

Storing

Place the turkey in a large, deep dish and cover it completely with clear film (plastic wrap). Keep it in the coolest part of the refrigerator, making sure that it (or any drip from the bird) does not come into contact with other foods.

TYPES OF TURKEY

Bronze birds

These are dark-feathered birds and the skin may be spotted with slightly dark stubble remaining after plucking. Norfolk Bronze is a popular breed and Norfolk Black is a very

plump-breasted bird. American Bronze is another traditional breed of turkey. Cambridge turkeys are also traditional in Britain and they have been crossed with American Bronze to breed the Cambridge Bronze.

White birds

In north America the White Holland is a popular breed of turkey. The majority of British turkeys are white, and traditional breeds include the Norfolk turkey. However, the superior-flavoured bronze and dark-feathered birds are becoming more popular, and more widely available.

Above: The majority of turkeys are white-feathered birds like this Norfolk turkey.

Free-range and/or organic birds

Both free-range and organic birds are available, and information on the rearing conditions is often provided. Birds that are labelled free-range should be checked carefully before buying, as this is not necessarily an indication of high quality. For the best turkey, seek out a source of organic birds from a known farm.

Cuts of turkey

As well as whole birds, there are a variety of prepared cuts of turkey available.

Part-boned breast This is a large roasting joint consisting of the whole breast, meat and bone, with skin on. Usually taken from large birds, these can weigh as much as a small turkey and provide a large number of portions. The joint can be stuffed under the skin. As well as a joint made up from the breast bone with meat on both sides, a breast fillet from one side, including the first part of the wing, can be removed from a whole turkey.

Boneless breast This is usually taken from one side of the breast, and neatly rolled or shaped with the skin around the outside. Quality varies – take care to distinguish between a boneless breast and a joint of "re-formed" meat, made up of scraps and off-cuts moulded into a joint under skin or a layer of fat.

Breast fillets These are skinless, boneless slices off the breast.

Turkey drumstick The leg of the bird is usually enough to provide a meal for four people with the right preparation. Turkey drumsticks have plenty of sinew running through the brown meat as well as fine bones. They can be roasted, but are better browned, then braised until the meat is succulent and tender, when they make full-flavoured casseroles.

Diced turkey Used mainly for pies and casseroles, this is often darker meat from the thigh or leg.

Stir-fry turkey These are long, thin strips of white breast meat.

Minced (ground) turkey This is good for pies, meat sauces and burgers or other recipes in which minced pork or beef would be used.

PREPARING TURKEY

Birds are usually sold cleaned and ready for stuffing or cooking. Methods of preparing small poultry apply to turkey, for example, trussing and tunnel boning are both relevant. The same rules also apply to hygiene when handling turkey. In addition, there are a few points to check before stuffing or roasting a large bird.

Singeing

Machine-plucking is not as thorough as old-fashioned hand-plucking, so birds tend to have more remnants of feathers. There are also areas of fine hair on the skin. Use tweezers to remove any remaining feathers. Then use a long lighted match to singe off any tiny feathers or hairs, allowing the smoke to burn away before drawing the flame across the surface of the skin. (Birds with dark plumage have dark "stubble", which may look slightly unpleasant, but these small pits from which the feathers have been removed will melt away during the roasting process.) However, if there is a vast quantity all over the skin the bird should be rejected before purchase.

Removing fat

Check inside the neck end of the bird for any lumps of excess fat and pull or cut them away.

Stuffing

Never stuff turkey in advance. The stuffing can be made in advance, but the turkey should not be stuffed until just before it is placed in the oven. Weigh the stuffing first, then add this to the weight of the bird for calculating the cooking time. Truss the bird, then cook for the calculated time; never shorten the cooking time because the meat appears cooked – time must be allowed for cooking the stuffing.

Introducing aromatics

The popular method and technique generally recommended, is to place aromatics in the body cavity and pack the stuffing under the skin covering the breast. Cut a large onion in half and stud each half with 4–6 cloves. Place this in the body cavity of the bird. Cut 1 orange and 1 lemon into quarters and add these with 3–4 bay leaves, 4–6 sage sprigs and 2–3 thyme sprigs. Add 1 cinnamon stick or 1 blade of mace for a festive hint of warm spice.

Stuffing the breast

This is the most popular method. Loosen the skin over the breast meat and insert stuffing underneath it. It is a good idea to introduce some stuffing here, even when stuffing the cavity, as this protects the delicate breast meat during long cooking.

Making stuffing

Stuffings, fillings and forcemeats are highly flavoured mixtures of ingredients. They are added to plain foods (fish, poultry, meat or vegetables) to introduce complex flavours. They can take any number of forms, but bound mixtures are popular. Minced (ground) meat, particularly veal, pork or sausage meat (bulk sausage), is a traditional main ingredient. Mixtures are also often based on breadcrumbs. Rice is also a popular base for stuffings. In contemporary recipes, the stuffing may not be bound into a mixture that can be spooned out easily, but consist of loose combinations of chopped fruits or vegetables.

Flavourings

The essence of a stuffing is the flavouring it brings to the bird, from herbs, spices and citrus fruit to strongly flavoured vegetables. The flavourings must complement, not compete with, the poultry or meat. The binding ingredients are, essentially, the carriers that bring a balance to the mixture and make it delicious to eat.

Making stuffing balls

Any stuffing that is not used to stuff the bird can be rolled into small balls about the size of walnuts. Place these in a separate baking tin (pan) or add them to the roasting pan, arranging them around the bird, for the final 15 minutes cooking time, and then serve with the carved meat and vegetables.

Stuffing the body cavity

Generally, stuffing can be prepared in advance and chilled separately from the bird but do not place in the bird until just before roasting. Weigh both bird and stuffing, then add the weights together to calculate the cooking time. Thoroughly rinse the body cavity under cold running water, then drain it well. (Remember to thoroughly wash the sink out afterwards.)

1 Wipe the turkey, inside and out, with kitchen paper.

2 Insert the sausagemeat stuffing, using your hands or a large spoon, but do not pack it in too tightly.

Stuffing the neck end

It is traditional to use two stuffings for turkey. Here sage and onion stuffing is used to fill the neck end of the bird. Before the stuffing is added, it is a good idea to remove the wishbone to make carving the breast easier.

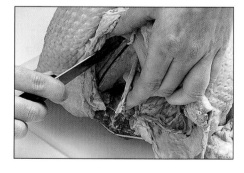

1 Fold back the flap of skin at the neck end and then use a small, sharp knife to cut out the wishbone, working right round the bone and cutting the meat as close to the bone as possible. Cut the bone free at the base on both sides.

2 Press the stuffing inside the shallow neck cavity.

3 Turn the bird over on to its breast and pull the neck skin over the stuffing.

4 Truss the bird to secure the flap of skin in place. If necessary, use a metal skewer to keep the skin in place while trussing the bird with string.

Herbs for sausage meat and chestnut stuffing

The stuffing for turkey is often left plain, especially when used in combination with sage and onion stuffing, but complementary herbs can be added. Try the following simple combinations:

Parsley and thyme Add 15ml/1 tbsp chopped fresh thyme and 45ml/ 3 tbsp chopped fresh parsley.

Tarragon and parsley Add 30ml/ 2 tbsp chopped fresh tarragon and 30ml/2 tbsp chopped fresh parsley.

Marjoram and orange Add 15ml/ 1 tbsp dried marjoram and the grated rind of 1 orange.

Sage and parsley Add 45ml/3 tbsp chopped fresh sage and 45ml/ 3 tbsp chopped fresh parsley.

Stuffings for turkey

Sausage meat and chestnut These are favourite ingredients for stuffing turkey. Buy sausage meat (bulk sausage) with a high proportion of meat. Use fresh chestnuts in season, or look for ready-prepared, vacuum-packed chestnuts.

1 Peel 900g/2lb fresh chestnuts, by slitting the peel and pulling it off. Remove the brown skin inside the shell. Cook the chestnuts in boiling water for 10–15 minutes. Drain well, then crumble the chestnuts into a large bowl.

2 Melt 25g/1oz butter in a large frying pan and add 2 finely chopped onions. Cook for 10 minutes, stirring occasionally until the onions are soft, but not browned.

3 Add the cooked onions to the chestnuts and mix well. Return the empty frying pan to the heat and then crumble in about 450g/1lb pork sausage meat.

4 Cook the mixture over a low to medium heat, stirring frequently, until the sausage meat is crumbly and well browned.

5 Add the sausage meat to the chestnut mixture with 115g/4oz fresh white breadcrumbs. Season and add chopped fresh herbs if required (see below left). Beat 1 egg and mix it into the stuffing to bind the ingredients.

Sage and onion This classic stuffing is suitable for all types of poultry, but especially with turkey.

1 Melt 25g/1oz butter in a frying pan. Add 4 finely chopped onions and cook for 10–15 minutes, until soft but not browned. Set aside to cool.

2 Add the onions to 115g/4oz fresh white breadcrumbs and 60ml/4 tbsp chopped fresh sage. Season, then add 1 beaten egg and about 125ml/ 4fl oz stock to bind the stuffing.

COOKING TURKEY

Roasting

Turkeys are easy to roast, but require a little more attention than smaller birds. Check that the oven shelves are in the correct position before heating the oven.

1 Put the prepared, stuffed bird on a rack in a large roasting pan.

2 Use a knife to generously smear the breast with butter (this helps to keep the meat moist). Season well with salt and freshly ground black pepper and place in the oven.

Thawing frozen turkey
Frozen turkey must be thawed completely before cooking. Unwrap the turkey and place it on a rack in a deep dish, so that the liquid that drips from the bird as it thaws runs below the rack and into the dish. Cover with clear film (plastic wrap) and refrigerate.
Thawing times
Allow 2–3 days in the refrigerator for a 4.5kg/10lb bird.
Allow 3–4 days in the refrigerator for a 6.8kg/15lb bird.

3 Baste the turkey frequently during the cooking time. When the breast has browned, cover the bird with foil and continue cooking and basting.

4 To check if the meat is cooked, insert a metal skewer into the thickest part of the thigh. If the juices run clear and the meat is white, it is cooked. If the juices run pink and the meat is soft and pink, the turkey is not ready, return it to the oven and check again after 20 minutes. Remove the foil for the final 20 minutes of cooking to finish browning the skin and give it a crisp texture.

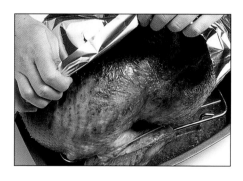

5 When the turkey is cooked, remove it from the oven and cover it closely with foil. Leave it to rest in a warm place for 15 minutes before carving. If you are going to make gravy, then transfer the turkey to a dish or carving tray.

Roasting times for turkey
Preheat the oven to 180°C/350°F/Gas 4. Calculate the cooking time, according to the weight of the bird (remember to weigh the bird and stuffing separately and add the two together, for total weight). Use the following as a guide to time, checking and basting regularly during cooking. It is difficult to estimate the exact cooking time when roasting large birds, as the shape and proportion of breast meat and the exact quantity and position of stuffing all influence the finished result.
For birds up to 4.5kg/10lb, allow 20 minutes per 450g/1lb plus an extra 20 minutes.
For birds over 4.5kg/10lb, allow 18 minutes per 450g/1lb, plus an extra 20 minutes.
For birds over 6.8kg/15lb, allow 15 minutes per 450g/1lb, plus an extra 20 minutes.

Carving turkey

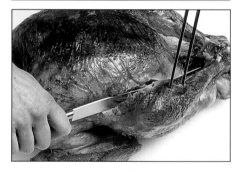

1 First remove the trussing string. Hold the bird steady in position with a carving fork. Cut off the legs from both sides of the bird, then cut these in half, or carve the meat from the bones.

2 Make a horizontal cut across the breast just above the wing.

3 Carve neat and even, vertical slices off the breast, then repeat on the other side. Arrange the slices of turkey on a warmed serving platter. Add the leg joints or meat to the platter or set them aside for serving separately.

Stir-frying turkey

Fillets of turkey breast are ideal for stir-frying. Thigh and leg meat can be slightly tough because it contains more sinew. Use turkey with Oriental-style ingredients or stir-fry the strips of meat with onions, mushrooms and a dash of sherry for a simple, lightly sauced dish. Flavour a "Western-style" stir-fry with chopped fresh herbs, such as tarragon, chives and parsley.

1 Cut the breast meat across the grain into thin, even strips. To save this preparation step, you can look out for ready-prepared packs of stir-fry turkey strips in the supermarket.

2 Heat a little oil in a wok or large, heavy frying pan. Sunflower, groundnut or corn oils are all suitable as they can be heated to a high temperature without smoking. Olive oil gives a good flavour, but it burns easily.

3 Stir-fry the turkey until golden brown. Cook the turkey in batches if necessary and remove the strips from the pan, continuing until all the pieces are browned. Stir-fry the vegetables in the same pan, then return the turkey to the pan to finish cooking for a few minutes before serving.

Pan-frying turkey

This is a useful method for cooking fillets of turkey breast or fine escalopes (US scallops). It is also the first stage for braising or casseroling turkey. Small, neat portions of turkey thigh are ideal for casseroles.

1 Heat a little olive oil in a frying pan. Add the turkey pieces and cook, turning occasionally, for about 15 minutes, or until the meat is golden on all sides.

2 Once the turkey has turned golden brown, season it well and reduce the heat, then cover the pan and continue cooking gently for 15–20 minutes, or until the meat is cooked through and succulent. Serve at once.

Stewing and braising

Prepared diced turkey or portions cut from the thigh are a good choice of turkey cuts for stewing or braising. Whole drumsticks can also be cooked by this method, which renders them succulent and flavoursome.

1 First brown the pieces of turkey as you would if pan-frying. Instead of using a frying pan, a flameproof casserole can be used for browning and simmering or oven cooking.

2 When the turkey pieces are browned, use a slotted spoon to remove them from the pan and set them aside.

3 Cook a selection of thickly sliced or coarsely chopped vegetables in the fat remaining in the casserole. As a simple base, try 1 coarsely chopped onion and 2 sliced carrots. Add other ingredients to taste: 1 sliced fennel bulb, 2 sliced celery sticks, 2 sliced garlic cloves, 1–2 bay leaves and sprigs of parsley, sage or thyme.

4 Replace the browned turkey portions and pour in enough stock just to cover them. Bring to simmering point, then reduce the heat and cover the pan. Simmer on the hob (stovetop) for about 1 hour or place in the oven at 180°C/350°F/Gas 4 for 1–1½ hours.

Wines to serve with turkey

The traditional wine-drinking rule that red wines are only served with red meat and white wine is reserved for poultry (and fish and shellfish) is being broken and the truth is that, nowadays, you can drink either red or white wine with turkey. It is simply a matter of personal preference.

Turkey is similar to chicken and you can drink some of the same wines with the bigger bird as you can with chicken and poussin. But turkey does have a slightly stronger flavour and it can take a fuller, fruitier wine, either red or white. Try a bright fruity red from the Côtes du Rhône or a big lightly oaked white Burgundy.

DUCK AND GOOSE

DUCK

In China, where ducks were probably first domesticated, some very prolific layers have long been appreciated for their eggs. The European types have descended from the mallard, as have North American varieties. The Peking duck, a type of mallard, is thought to have been one of the original breeds from which the American Long Island ducks are descended. The barbary, or muscovy, duck is another ancient breed from which today's birds have evolved.

American Long Island and British Aylesbury ducks have a deep, rich flavour and a significant proportion of fat. The barbary duck and the Nantes duck (popular in France) have slightly less fat. The barbary is a big bird providing a good portion of firm breast meat. The Nantes is smaller, more tender and with a delicate flavour.

Below: Geese have defied all attempts to rear them intensively, and so these birds are one of the few remaining truly seasonal foods.

Left: Aylesbury duck, which has pale, tender meat.

Above: Barbary duck has less fat than other breeds.

The Rouen duck is more like game than duck in both taste and texture. This is due to the method by which they are slaughtered and the traditional method of cooking the bird. They are killed by being smothered to avoid loss of blood, then plucked while still warm, encouraging the blood to rush to the breast meat, making it particularly dark. The breasts are removed and lightly cooked while the remainder of the carcass is grilled (broiled), then pressed to remove any juices that it contains. These juices are the base for a rich sauce which is served on the rare breast meat.

Modern breeding and feeding methods have brought leaner ducks to the supermarket, with a good proportion of breast meat and only a fine layer of fat under the skin. The majority are ducklings, less than two months old. As well as whole birds, portions and breast fillets are readily available.

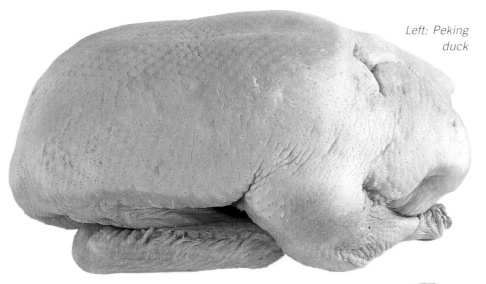

Left: Peking duck

GOOSE – A SEASONAL BIRD

Unlike other domesticated poultry and animals, the goose has defied the instigators of intensive rearing methods. Geese are not prolific layers and they are one of the few remaining sources of seasonal food. This large, fatty bird traditionally survived by pecking about and foraging for any available food. Found on poor farms because it was economical to keep and a good source of meat or fat, a special bird would be fattened for Christmas. It is the traditional celebration bird and has always been seen as a treat; a bird for both the poor and the rich.

In Britain, green goose was the young goose, so named because it had been fed off grass, rather than the stubble left in the fields after harvesting.

Above: Duck breast and a leg portion

Green goose was traditional for Michaelmas in September – country people thought that eating goose on Michaelmas day brought good luck for the rest of the year. The second season for goose was, of course, Christmas, when fattened, older birds were served.

Goose fat had all manner of uses; it was used by country people for rubbing into the chest to ward off colds and other household uses as well as for cooking. Preserved goose, the French *confit d'oie*, is the thoroughly stewed and rendered goose preserved in its own fat. Across central and Eastern Europe as well as Scandinavia, goose and goose fat are traditional in cooking. The most popular variety of bird is the Canada goose which, at 2.75kg/6lb, serves six people. The smaller greylag and even smaller pinkfoot are both well-flavoured birds. The smallest goose is the whitefront, which weighs about 2.5kg/5½lb in feather.

Nutrition

Duck and goose are high-protein foods. They also contain B-group vitamins and some minerals. Being high in fat, duck and goose should not feature frequently in the healthy diet, but they are excellent for special meals.

Buying

Look for light-skinned, plump birds. They should be soft and moist with no blemishes, bruises or feathers. The bird should smell fresh. Goose is seasonal and is also available frozen.

Storing

Cover the bird loosely with some baking parchment and keep on a deep tray in the bottom of the refrigerator so that the meat juices don't spill on to and contaminate other foods. The best and safest way to thaw a frozen duck or goose is slowly, in the refrigerator.

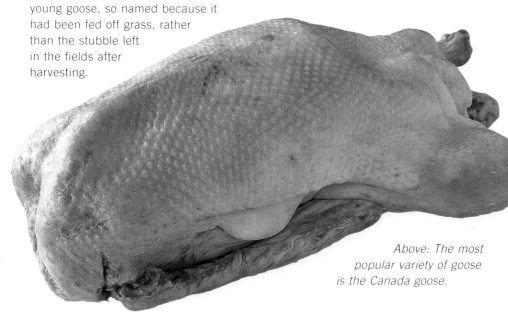

Above: The most popular variety of goose is the Canada goose.

PREPARING DUCK AND GOOSE

Duck and goose are sold prepared and ready for the oven. When buying a whole bird, remember that most are sold complete with giblets, packed in a small plastic pouch and placed in the body cavity – remember to remove these before roasting the bird (they can be used to make a rich gravy; see the section on gravies for instructions).

Jointing a duck

Ducks have a higher proportion of bone to meat than chicken. Therefore, rather than following the contours of the joints, as when preparing chicken portions, it is best to cut the bird into four equal-size pieces, allocating a good amount of meat to bone on each piece. Poultry shears and good, sharp knives are essential equipment for jointing birds.

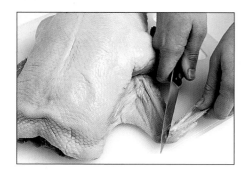

1 Use a small, sharp knife or poultry shears to trim the wing tips.

2 Carefully fold back the skin at the neck end and, using a small knife, cut out the wishbone.

3 Use poultry shears to cut the breast in half from the tail to the neck. Split the breastbone with the shears as neatly as possible.

4 Separate the bird in half by cutting along each side of the backbone, then remove the backbone.

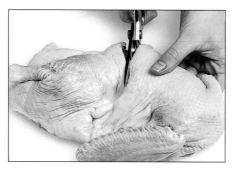

5 Cut each portion in half again. Cut diagonally to share the portion of meat equally between the 4 portions. This can be awkward – it's easier to cut through the flesh first, then the bone.

Boning duck breasts

Sometimes known as *margrets*, from the French name for them, boneless duck breast portions have a much stronger flavour than chicken breast portions and the meat is richer and darker. Duck breasts are a good choice if you enjoy the meat's rich flavour, but want to have as little as possible.

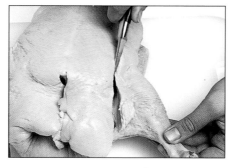

1 Use a sharp knife to cut the legs and thighs off the duck.

2 Place the duck on a chopping board. Cut along the breastbone on one side, working down the middle of the duck.

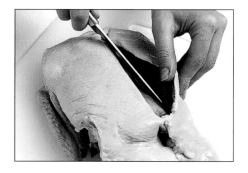

3 Gradually cut the breast meat off the bone on one side of the carcass.

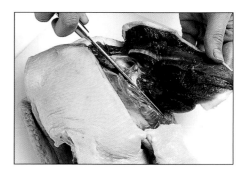

4 Lift the breast meat away as you cut it free from the carcass. Repeat on the opposite side of the carcass.

5 Turn the breast skin-side down on the board and cut out any sinews that run along the meat.

6 One way of finishing the breast before cooking is to lightly score the skin and fat in a diamond pattern, using a sharp knife. This allows the fat to escape and gives the cooked duck breast portion an attractive appearance, crisp skin and well-flavoured flesh.

Rendering duck or goose fat

Duck and goose fat are excellent for frying because they can be heated to a high temperature without burning. Potatoes fried or roasted in a little duck or goose fat become crisp and golden, as well as full-flavoured.

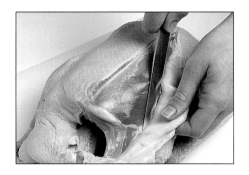

1 Cut the skin off the duck and trim all the excess fat from the bird.

2 Cut the skin and fat into small pieces and put in a pan with 200ml/7fl oz/ scant 1 cup cold water.

3 Heat until simmering, then reduce the heat to very low and cook, uncovered, for 1½ hours or until the fat has all melted down. Strain the fat through a fine sieve and leave to cool. Then store the fat in a covered container in the refrigerator and use for frying.

COOKING DUCK AND GOOSE

These are fatty birds, with dark meat that has plenty of flavour. The fat helps to keep the meat moist during cooking. Goose is almost always roasted, though the legs may be added to casseroles. Ducks are generally roasted whole, or cut up for frying or casseroling.

Roasting duck and goose

When roasting duck, remember that an average duck will not yield a high proportion of breast meat when carved, so unless the bird is to be jointed into sections when cooked, it is usual to roast two small ducks to serve four people. Goose does not yield a high proportion of meat and a 4.5kg/10lb goose will serve eight to ten people.

1 Stuff the bird if required, then truss it. Sage and onion stuffing is a classic choice for both duck and goose.

2 Season well and smear a little butter over the bird. This enriches the flesh and helps give the bird a golden colour.

3 Put the bird on a rack in a roasting pan (the excess fat will drip into the pan). Roast the duck for the calculated time. Turn and baste the bird frequently to keep the skin and flesh moist.

Roasting times for duck and goose
Preheat the oven to 180°C/350°F/ Gas 4. Weigh the bird and calculate the cooking time, allowing about 30 minutes per 450g/1lb for duck and 15–20 minutes per 450g/1lb for goose. To crisp the skin, raise the temperature to 200°C/400°F/ Gas 6 for the last 30 minutes.

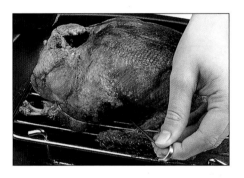

4 To check if the bird is cooked, insert a skewer into the thickest part of the thigh. If the juices run clear, the duck is cooked. If the juices are pink, the bird is not cooked.

5 Cover the roast bird tightly with foil and leave it to rest in a warm place, where it will not continue cooking. A warm grill (broiler) compartment is suitable (without the heat on). Allow 10–15 minutes for the temperature to become even throughout the meat.

Wines to serve with duck or goose
Try a soft, medium fruity red with roast duck – for example a Chilean Merlot. A claret (Bordeaux) or a Beaujolais also goes well with duck, especially roast or casseroled duck served in a fruit sauce. Vouvray, a medium white wine from the Loire, which has a wonderful crisp acidity, is a good choice for matching tart sauces, such as orange. Hearty roast goose could take a full-bodied red, such as a mature Burgundy, Côtes du Rhône, Côte-Rôtie or Chateauneuf-du-Pape.

Carving roast duck or goose

A small duck of up to 2.5kg/5½lb can be halved or quartered; the meat from a larger duck can be carved into neat slices. A goose can be carved as for a duck and the breast meat cut into slices.

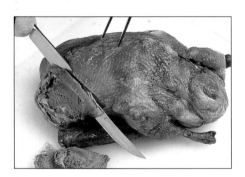

1 Cut the skin between the legs and the body, pushing the legs out with the blade of the knife to reveal the breast meat.

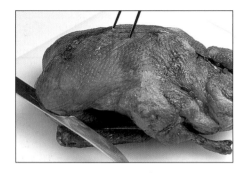

2 Make a horizontal cut just above the wing joint, through the breast meat to the bone. (If the wishbone has not yet been removed, cut it out.)

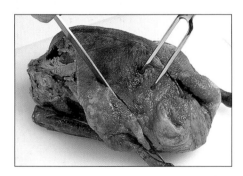

3 Carve long, neat slices off the breast, working at an angle to give diagonal slices. This provides the largest number of slices from each breast. (Alternatively cut slices the full length of the bird, parallel to the rib cage.)

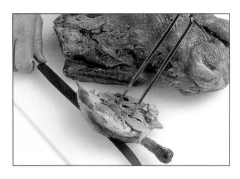

4 To remove the legs, turn the bird on its side and push the fork through the thigh. Force the leg outwards to break the joint that is located under the bird. Cut the leg off. Repeat on the other side. Cut the leg portions in half through the joint.

Grilling duck

1 Preheat the grill (broiler) to its hottest setting. Season the duck breast portions well. If it is important to remove as much fat as possible during cooking, prick the skin all over with a fork. Leaving the skin whole tends to keep the meat moist during cooking.

2 Place the breasts skin-side up on the rack of a grill pan.

3 Cook for 4–7 minutes, turning once, until well browned on both sides.

Pan-frying duck

Duck has a high fat content and it is well suited to dry-frying, without the addition of any extra fat.

1 Heat a heavy frying pan or flat or ridged griddle until hot. Put the duck breast portions in the dry pan, skin-side down. Don't overcrowd the pan; cook the meat in batches if necessary.

2 Cook over a medium heat for about 4 minutes, pressing down using a palette knife or metal spatula to keep the breast flat and to force out all the fat from the skin.

3 Turn the duck breast portions over using tongs, and cook for 3–4 minutes on the second side. When cooked, the breasts should be slightly firm and still quite pink in the centre.

4 Remove from the pan and place on a plate. Cover with foil and leave to rest in a warm place for 5 minutes.

5 Use a sharp knife to cut the breast portions into neat slices, working at an angle of about 45º.

Stir-frying duck

Sharp and sour flavours go well with stir-fried duck and are popular in Oriental dishes. Skinless, boneless breast meat is suitable for this method of cooking. Although duck breast meat is fairly expensive, it is a rich-tasting meat and stir-frying is a good way of making a little meat go a long way.

1 For quick, even cooking, the duck meat must be cut into thin strips. Use a large, sharp knife and slice the meat crossways into even-size pieces.

2 Add just a little oil to a wok or frying pan. Use groundnut, sunflower, corn or vegetable oil, which can be heated to a high temperature without burning.

3 When the oil is very hot, add the duck and stir-fry over a medium to high heat for 2–3 minutes, or until tender.

Casseroling duck

There are many traditional recipes for duck casseroles and they were often greasy dishes. With the leaner duck available today, there is no reason to have a fatty result.

1 Brown the duck portions well first; if your casserole isn't large enough to fit the duck pieces in one layer, then do this in a heavy frying pan. Drain off all but a little fat before adding and softening the vegetables.

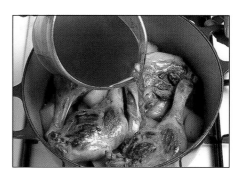

2 Transfer the vegetables and duck (or return the duck) to the casserole and pour in the liquid. This can be stock, red or white wine, or (hard) cider. Bring to the boil, then transfer the casserole to the oven and cook at 180ºC/350ºF/Gas 4 for 1½ hours. Alternatively, simmer gently on the hob (stovetop). Before serving, skim off any fat and season.

Accompaniments to serve with duck and goose

Oranges and sharp cherries complement these rich poultry and are popular for flavouring sauces. Sharp apple sauce is also traditional. Cranberry sauce goes well with both duck and goose. Goose is traditionally stuffed with chestnuts and apples, pears and quinces. Plum or gooseberry compotes also go well with goose. Fresh herb and onion sauces and dressings are favourite accompaniments in America and Canada. Fresh peas are a classic vegetable for serving with duck. Sage, thyme, rosemary and mint are good herbs for duck.

Sharp and sweet flavours go well with fatty meats, cutting their richness. Dried fruit, such as prunes and apricots, are good examples, especially when combined with spirits, such as brandy, or fortified wine, such as port. Fresh green flavours also balance them well – chives, spring onions (scallions), rocket (arugula) and tarragon are excellent ingredients for pepping up sauces or reduced roasting juices boiled with a little wine.

GAME BIRDS

Although game birds are shot for sport, historically they are a major source of food. Until recently, there seemed to be no end to the wild birds that could be acquired for the pot, but the fact that some species were in danger of becoming extinct

Above: Pheasants are the most plentiful of game birds and are often sold in a brace: a pair of birds that includes the smaller hen and a cock.

Below: Oven-ready cock (top) and hen pheasants.

eventually led to the introduction of conservation laws and hunting seasons in many countries. Today, game birds are protected by law.

There are "closed" seasons when game cannot be killed to allow them to grow in number again. Fresh game is only available in shops during the hunting season, but in some countries frozen game is stocked throughout the year. The seasons vary slightly from state to state in north America and from country to country in the rest of the world. In Britain, grouse, ptarmigan and snipe can only be shot between 12th August (the Glorious Twelfth), and 10th December (or 31st January in the case of snipe). The season for partridge normally runs from 1st September to 1st February, and for pheasant from 1st October to 1st February.

Tradition, myth and mystery surround game to such an extent that many people are swayed from sampling the birds. They are now sold prepared and ready for the oven, and are no more difficult to cook than chicken, turkey or goose. Young birds are best roasted but older birds benefit from long, slow cooking for tender results.

Nutrition

Feathered game is a high-quality protein food in the same sense as poultry. The advantage it has over most farmed meat and poultry is that it is low in fat and free from additives.

Buying

Larger supermarkets offer a good choice of game in season. Specialist butchers offer a wider choice, frozen products and extensive advice. A butcher who specializes in game will be able to tell you the age and the sex of the bird, and give you useful cooking information, too.

Left: The magnificent Capercaillie, which was hunted to extinction in Britiain in the late 18th century.

Game birds do not look quite as perfect as poultry. They often look a little damaged, and they may have the odd tear in the skin, but they should not be seriously injured. Limbs should be intact, never broken. Pheasant should be even in shape with no serious shot damage (see checking for shot opposite) with a strong, but pleasant aroma. Partridge should be plump, with an obvious smell of game and soft, pale flesh. When buying grouse, look for moist, fresh skin, deep, red flesh and no serious shot damage. Fresh quail should have a good round shape and plump flesh – a bird with a high proportion of meaty flesh to bone.

Above: Red-legged (left) and grey-legged partridges are two different species – the grey-legged is generally smaller.

Storing

Birds that are sold pre-packed should be left in their packing and used by the date on the packet. Place loose birds in a deep dish and cover with clear film (plastic wrap). Store in the coldest part of the refrigerator. A bird that has been hung and is ready for cooking can be kept for one to two days or it can be frozen.

Checking for shot

Unfortunately, tiny balls of lead shot are left in game birds. Rub your fingertips over the surface of the game to try to locate any small hard balls, and then cut them out. Always warn those who are eating the dish to be aware that the bird may contain shot.

TYPES OF FEATHERED GAME

Pheasant

By far the most plentiful and popular of game birds, pheasant was originally introduced to Europe from China. Pheasant are often sold in pairs, a male and female, known as a brace. The hen is more tender and smaller than the cock and it will serve three people, while the cock will serve four.

Above: Oven-ready, red-legged and grey-legged partridges. The smaller, grey-legged bird (bottom) is considered to have a superior flavour.

Right: Mallard is the largest wild duck and should serve two or three people.

Pheasant is excellent for roasting or stewing: roast a young bird and stew an older fowl.

Grouse

Native to Scotland, where grouse is regarded as the king of feathered game, it has a wonderful, rich flavour from feeding on highland heather. One bird provides a good single portion. While young birds are usually roasted or grilled (broiled), older birds are cooked in a casserole. Complicated recipes for grouse are few and far between because this bird is best prepared simply.

Partridge

There are two main types of partridge, the French or red-legged partridge, which was introduced into England in 1673, and the indigenous English or grey-legged partridge. The red-legged bird is bigger but the flavour of the grey bird is often preferred. Partridge can be roasted, stewed or braised. Young birds are best roasted and served in their own cooking juices. Partridge is not very big: serve one per person.

Wild duck

This is far less fatty than domesticated duck, which is important when you come to cook it. Generally, most recipes for duck can be adapted for either bird, but it may be necessary to add a little fat when cooking the game bird. Duck taken from inland water is usually preferable to that from salty water (the latter tend to have a slightly fishy flavour). Plump **mallard** is the largest and most common of all the

Above: Wigeon

Below: Oven-ready wigeon

Below: Oven-ready teal

wild ducks. It is more intense in flavour than domesticated duck and is excellent for roasting. One bird serves two to three people. **Teal** is one of the smallest wild ducks and is highly prized by gourmets, and **canvasback**, **wigeon**, **gadwall**, **pintail** and **pochard** are also available. Young birds are generally tender but older ones can be quite tough and in need of long, slow cooking in a casserole.

Wild goose

The Canada goose (which averages about 4.75kg/10½lb in feather or 2.75kg/6lb dressed) is one of the plumpest and tastiest of geese and it serves six people. The smaller greylag (3.8kg/8½lb in feather) and the even smaller pinkfoot (2.7kg/6lb in feather) are also good on the plate. The smallest wild goose you are likely to come across is the whitefront (2.5kg/5½lb in feather). Roast a wild goose in the same way as a domesticated goose. As with wild duck, try to avoid those wild geese from salty water; birds that have been feeding on grass or stubble taste much better than those that have been living and eating on marshland. Also avoid birds over a year old, as these are not considered good enough to eat.

Quail

Native to the Middle East, where there are many different varieties of this small bird, quail are available all the year round. They are very small birds, and one provides an appetizer or two make a main-course portion per person.

Pigeon

Cheap, plentiful and available all the year round. The pigeon is found wild all over the world, yet has never been held in particularly high esteem, but it is surprisingly tasty. Wood pigeons are meaty birds, and usually about 450g/1lb in weight.

Above: Quail

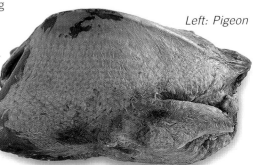

Left: Pigeon

Serve one per person. Pigeons can be braised, cooked in a salmis, where the birds are first roasted, then finished in a sauce, or they can be turned into pigeon pie.

Squab

This is a young pigeon, and these small birds are now reared commercially for eating, although they are usually only available in the spring. Squabs weigh about 350g/12oz. They have meaty breasts and are more tender than older, wild pigeons, and so they can be simply larded with bacon or pork fat and then

Small birds

Coot, corncrake, moorhen and rail are marsh birds from around the world. With the exception of corncrake, they are not prized for their flavour. The corncrake (also known as a land rail) often leaves the marshes for the fields, which explains its superior flavour.

The stockdove, rock dove (ancestor of the domestic pigeon) and turtle dove have never been as popular as the wood pigeon. Lark, plover, thrush, hazel hen and mud hen are treated as game birds in some countries.

Right: Woodcock

Left: Woodcock is a tiny bird with a plump, meaty breast and is highly prized for its flavour. It can be roasted, braised or grilled.

roasted at a fairly low temperature for about an hour, and served with the flesh still pink. They can also be braised, or split in half and grilled (broiled).

Woodcock

This long-beaked bird has a wonderful, rich flavour. Woodcock can be roasted, braised, grilled or broiled. It is a small bird, so one is usually served per person. When the birds are roasted it is usual to leave the innards intact as this is thought to add to the flavour. The innards or "trail" can be eaten – usually spread on toast, and served with the bird. The head is left on, but skinned and is often split after cooking as many gourmets regard the brain as quite a delicacy.

Snipe

This is a tiny, long-legged marsh bird with a very long beak. Like the woodcock, it is seldom for sale in butchers' or game dealers' stores; you are more likely to come across snipe if you, or someone you know, shoot. It is best roasted, although some are so small that they can also be grilled – split the birds in half and flatten them first. Serve one or two per person.

Above: Snipe is more likely to come your way if you or your friends shoot.

Capercaillie

This magnificent bird, which weighs about 4kg/9lb, resembles a very large grouse. It was hunted to extinction in Britain by the end of the 18th century. Nowadays, it is found in the mountainous regions of northern Europe and has been reintroduced to Scotland, but it is a forest forager and has an inferior flavour compared to grouse.

Ptarmigan

This member of the grouse family is called rock ptarmigan in North America. It is very rarely seen (or shot) because its preferred habitat is a high, stony mountainside. The flavour of the meat varies according to the wild foods that the bird has been eating, but it is somewhat similar to that of other grouse.

Below: Snipe, prepared ready for cooking.

Above: Squab, which is a baby pigeon reared especially for the table, is a perfect individual portion and is best cooked and served whole.

PREPARING GAME BIRDS

Game is sold hung, feathered, drawn and ready for cooking. Specialist butchers will advise on game which has been hung for a short time and is light in flavour, or they will hang game for a longer period, on request, to develop a more intense flavour. Plucking and hanging are not practical techniques for home preparation; the former is messy and can be done in an outbuilding, but, to avoid rotting game, it must be hung in suitably cool, dry and airy conditions which encourage it to mature without extensive rotting. Should you have feathered game, your local specialist butcher will probably be prepared to hang and pluck the bird for you.

Trussing a pheasant

This helps keep the bird in shape during cooking.

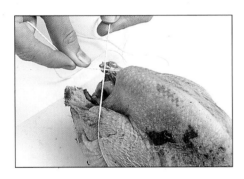

1 Season the bird well. Take a piece of string around the wing joints and bring both ends forward across the thighs. Cross the ends over.

2 Wrap the string tightly around the thighbones, then cross the ends. Pull the string under the parson's nose and tie it neatly. Tuck the ends of the thighbones neatly into the cavity.

Jointing a grouse for casseroling

When repeated on both sides, jointing produces two wings, two breasts, two thighs and two drumsticks.

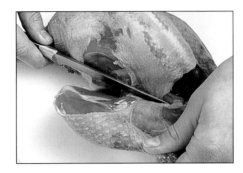

1 Using a sharp knife, remove one leg from the bird by cutting through the skin and then through the thigh joint. Repeat on the other side.

2 Using a pair of poultry shears, or sharp, kitchen scissors, cut the breast in half, splitting the breastbone.

3 Turn the bird over and then cut out the backbone using poultry shears or scissors. Leave the wings attached to the breast portions.

4 Using the poultry shears, cut each breast in half diagonally so that one piece of breast is attached to the wing.

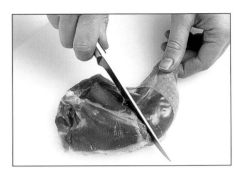

5 Using a sharp knife, cut each leg in half through the knee joint.

6 Cut off the wing tip at the first joint.

Spatchcocking a pigeon or wild duck

If you want to grill (broil) small birds it is best to spatchcock them (split and open them out flat) first to ensure that they cook evenly. The following method is essentially the same as for poultry, but it is a good idea to remember to handle smaller game birds gently to avoid damage.

1 Tuck the wings under the bird and remove the wishbone using a small, sharp knife.

2 Turn the bird over and use poultry shears or a large sharp knife to cut along each side of the backbone.

3 Remove the backbone from the bird.

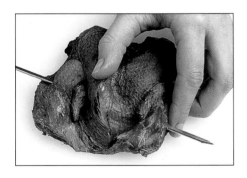

4 Put the bird on a chopping board and push down hard with your fist to break the breastbone.

5 With the bird pressed flat, push a skewer through the wings and breast.

6 Push a second metal skewer through the thighs.

COOKING GAME BIRDS

Simple cooking methods are often the best for game; plain roasting for tender birds and simple casserole cooking for those that are tougher.

Roasting

With the exception of restaurant facilities, spit-roasting has been replaced by practical oven methods. Lean game birds should be basted frequently or larded with fatty bacon before roasting to keep them tender.

1 Season the bird and cover it evenly with streaky (fatty) bacon.

2 Put the bird on a rack in a roasting pan and place in the preheated oven.

3 Baste the bird frequently to keep it moist and succulent during cooking.

4 To check if the bird is cooked, use a metal skewer to pierce the meat at the thickest part of the thigh. If there are any signs of blood in the juices, the bird is not cooked.

5 Cover the bird closely with foil and set it aside to rest in a warm place for 5–10 minutes before carving.

> **Roasting times for game birds**
> Game birds are always roasted quickly at a high temperature. Prepare the bird or birds as described above, then weigh and calculate the cooking time. Baste frequently during cooking.
> **Pheasant** Allow 30–45 minutes at 230°C/450°F/Gas 8.
> **Grouse** 20–30 minutes at 230°C/450°F/Gas 8.
> **Partridge** 15–20 minutes at 240°C/475°F/Gas 9.
> **Quail** 18–20 minutes at 220°C/425°F/Gas 7.
> **Pigeon** 15–20 minutes at 240°C/475°F/Gas 9.
> **Woodcock** 15–18 minutes at 240°C/475°F/Gas 9.
> **Snipe** 10–15 minutes at 240°C/475°F/Gas 9.

Carving game birds

Let the bird rest in a warm place for a few minutes before carving.

1 Remove the bacon used to bard the bird and cut off the trussing string.

2 Cut through the skin on either side of the bird and cut off both the legs.

3 Carve off the breast meat in neat vertical slices. Repeat on the other side.

Accompaniments to serve with game birds
Fried breadcrumbs Fresh white breadcrumbs fried in a little butter until crisp and golden.
Game chips These thinly sliced, deep-fried potatoes are the classic accompaniment for game birds.
Roast parsnips Par-boiled parsnips, rolled in a little flour and drizzled with melted butter, then finished in a hot oven until tender and golden.
Sauces Cumberland sauce and bread sauce are traditional accompaniments.
Fruit jellies Crab apple, rowanberry, redcurrant or other fruit jellies are excellent with roast game.

Grilling

This is an ideal cooking method for smaller birds such as quail. If grilling (broiling) larger birds such as squab, then split them and open out flat to reduce the height and ensure they cook evenly.

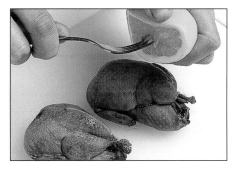

1 Preheat the grill (broiler) to high. Brush the birds lightly with olive oil and squeeze a little lemon juice over the top. Season with salt and plenty of freshly ground black pepper.

2 Put the birds on the rack in a grill pan. Grill under a medium to high heat for 5–6 minutes, or until well browned. Turn the birds over and cook the second side until browned.

3 When cooked, the breast meat of the birds should be still slightly pink and juicy in the middle.

Pan-frying pigeon breasts

Pigeon breast portions, which have been pan-fried, can be served with a sauce or salad. This is also the first stage for a sauced dish. For example, remove the browned breasts and add mushrooms and chopped spring onions (scallions). Sauté the vegetables for 2 minutes. Add 250ml/8fl oz/1 cup Madeira and bring to the boil. Boil rapidly for about 30 seconds, then replace the breasts and reduce the heat. Cook gently for 2–3 minutes, season and serve.

1 Heat a frying pan until hot, then add a little vegetable oil and heat again.

2 Add the pigeon breast portions and cook until browned underneath.

3 Turn the breast portions and cook until well browned on the second side.

Casseroling

Male birds and older game birds are ideal for casseroles.

Once the pieces of game bird are fully browned, basic vegetables (sliced or coarsely chopped onion, carrot, celery) should be added to the casserole along with a bouquet garni, then red wine or rich stock poured in. Bring the liquid to simmering point, then transfer the casserole to a preheated oven at 180°C/ 350°F/Gas 4 and cook for 1½ hours. Add sliced mushrooms and a selection of wild mushrooms and cook for a further 15 minutes. Taste and season before serving. The cooking juices may be thickened with beurre manié and enriched with a little double (heavy) cream before serving.

Marinades for game birds

These moisten and flavour game birds, and also help to tenderize the meat and enhance its flavour. Place the whole bird or pieces in a deep, non-metallic bowl or dish, pour over the marinade and leave birds or pieces to marinate for several hours in a cool place or overnight in the refrigerator. Try one of the following combinations for game birds:
• Fresh orange juice, with grated lime rind and cracked peppercorns.
• Red wine with cranberry juice and juniper berries.
• White wine with allspice berries and a cinnamon stick.
• Fresh pineapple juice with grated lemon rind.

Pot-roasting

This is a good method for slightly dry game birds, such as a cock pheasant.

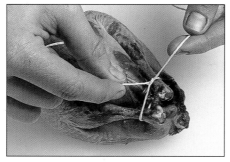

1 Tuck the neck skin and wings under the bird and then tie the legs together with string.

2 Season the bird well with salt and pepper. Wrap rashers of streaky (fatty) bacon around the bird, and then tie them in place with string.

3 Heat about 15ml/1 tbsp oil in a large, flameproof casserole. Add the bird and brown it gently, turning occasionally.

COOK'S TIP

If you don't have a casserole that can be used on the hob, brown the birds and vegetables in a frying pan and transfer to a casserole for cooking in the oven.

Wines to serve with game birds

Full-flavoured reds go well with rich game. Try a fine claret from Bordeaux or a good bottle from the Rhône. Older, earthy Burgundies complement roast or casseroled pheasant. Soft, fruity mature reds such as Australian Grenache go well with roast partridge. Try Chianti Classico with quail. Some of the better regional French wines – Fitou, Bergerac or the better reds from the Loire Valley – complement all game birds.

4 Remove the bird from the casserole and keep warm. Add diced carrots and chopped onions with salt and pepper to taste to the casserole. Sweat the vegetables in the juices remaining in the casserole for a few minutes.

5 Return the bird to the casserole and pour over enough red wine to half-cover the bird. Bring to the boil, then reduce the heat until the liquid is just simmering. Cook gently for about 30 minutes on the hob (stovetop) or 1 hour in the oven at 180°C/350°F/Gas 4, or until the sauce is reduced and the bird is cooked through.

FURRED GAME

The traditional definition of furred game was any animal killed for sport (or game) but the historical importance was as a source of food. In fact, furred game has been hunted and killed for food since prehistoric times. Long before man learned to cultivate crops and to domesticate sheep, goats, pigs and cattle, ancient man hunted small birds and animals to supplement his diet of wild fruit and root vegetables. In practically every part of the world, game – whether big game such as reindeer, elk, moose, antelope, wild boar and even bear, or small game such as rabbit, hare and squirrel – has been a vital part of the human diet for as long as man has been eating meat.

In the kitchen, game means any edible animal not raised on the farm, although, nowadays, furred game such as deer and rabbit can be farmed. The most common furred game eaten all over the world includes deer, rabbit, hare and wild boar.

Nutrition

Furred game is exceptionally nutritious meat. It is high in protein, low in cholesterol and particularly low in fat.

Buying

If you hunt or shoot, you may not need to buy furred game, but, generally, most people get game from a shop. Rabbit and some joints of venison are finding their way on to the supermarket shelf, but the best place to buy furred game is at a specialist butcher. It is here that you will get a good choice of animals and their different cuts, and also the benefit of expert advice.

Venison should have been properly hung to give the meat time to become tender. It is naturally lean, but don't be afraid of a little fat as this helps bring out the flavour of the meat and will keep it moist and juicy as it cooks.

When you buy wild boar, look for firm, pink flesh, which is moist but not damp or oily. The fat should be white,

Above: Moose, which is hunted in North America, is a large member of the deer family, and is similar to European elk.

not yellow, and the bones should be tinged with red. The skin should be dry and silky, not slimy or damp.

Rabbit and hare should have an even covering of flesh, a rounded back and lean, moist pale-pink flesh

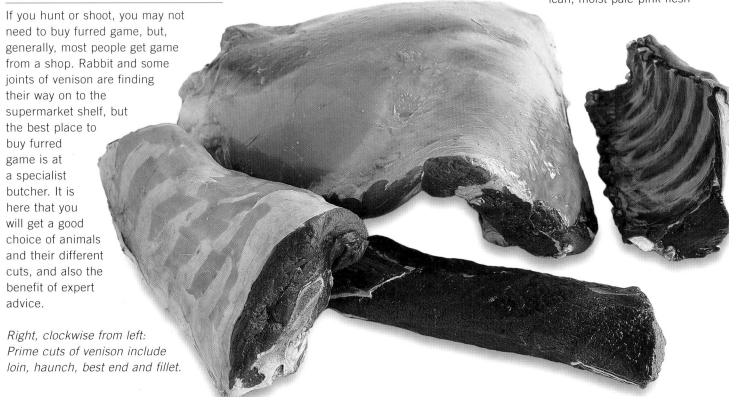

Right, clockwise from left: Prime cuts of venison include loin, haunch, best end and fillet.

and benefit from long cooking to bring out the flavour of the meat. It is not actually the type or size of the deer that matters but what the animal has been feeding on: if, for example, it has been grazing on heather and acorns, it will be full of flavour. **Red deer** originally lived in the forests of northern Europe and they still live wild in the Highlands of Scotland (in areas that even now are known as deer forests although there is hardly a tree in sight). The red deer is the largest and is related to species in North Africa and Asia. **Fallow deer** are descended from those herds that lived in the deer parks on the great country estates. The **roe deer** is smaller than the red deer and the fallow deer but has the finest flavoured meat.

Muntjac, which is known as pig deer in Europe and barking deer in South-east Asia,

Above, from left: Venison cuts that benefit from long, slow cooking include neck, shoulder and shin.

with very little visible fat. Avoid carcasses that show signs of injury or disease or which have been clumsily shot. Rabbit can be bought all the year round as it may be farmed or wild rabbit. Fresh wild hares are available in late autumn and winter; the exact dates vary from country to country. If you are preparing jugged hare and need the blood to thicken the sauce, ask your butcher to collect it for you.

Storing

Remove any packaging from the meat, wrap it in baking parchment and put it on a small tray. Store in the bottom of the refrigerator, so that it can't drip on to cooked meats or other foods. Meat that is ready for cooking can be stored for one to two days in the refrigerator or it can be frozen.

TYPES OF FURRED GAME

Deer

The word venison was originally used to describe the meat of any furred animal killed in the chase for food, including wild boar, rabbit and hare as well as

Above: Red deer haunch

deer. Today, in Britain and Australia, the word simply means the meat from deer; although in America it is used, more broadly, to include meat from elk, moose, reindeer, caribou and antelope.

Venison is a dark, close-textured meat with very little fat; what there is should be firm and white. If it is in good condition and a prime cut, such as haunch, loin, fillet or best end, it will be juicy and tender and is best served rare. Other cuts, such as neck, shoulder and shin (shank), are often marinated

is even smaller and is largely feral in Britain, so can be shot as vermin (when farmers report damage to crops) at any time.

The **white-tailed** or **Virginian deer** is the plentiful deer of North America and is hunted on the eastern seaboard.

Reindeer live in northern Europe and Asia, and, as well as giving Father Christmas a lift from Lapland around the world once a year, makes a popular meat dish in Finland, Sweden and Russia. Its close relation, **caribou**, has always played an important part in the diet of those living in Alaska and other frozen parts of North America.

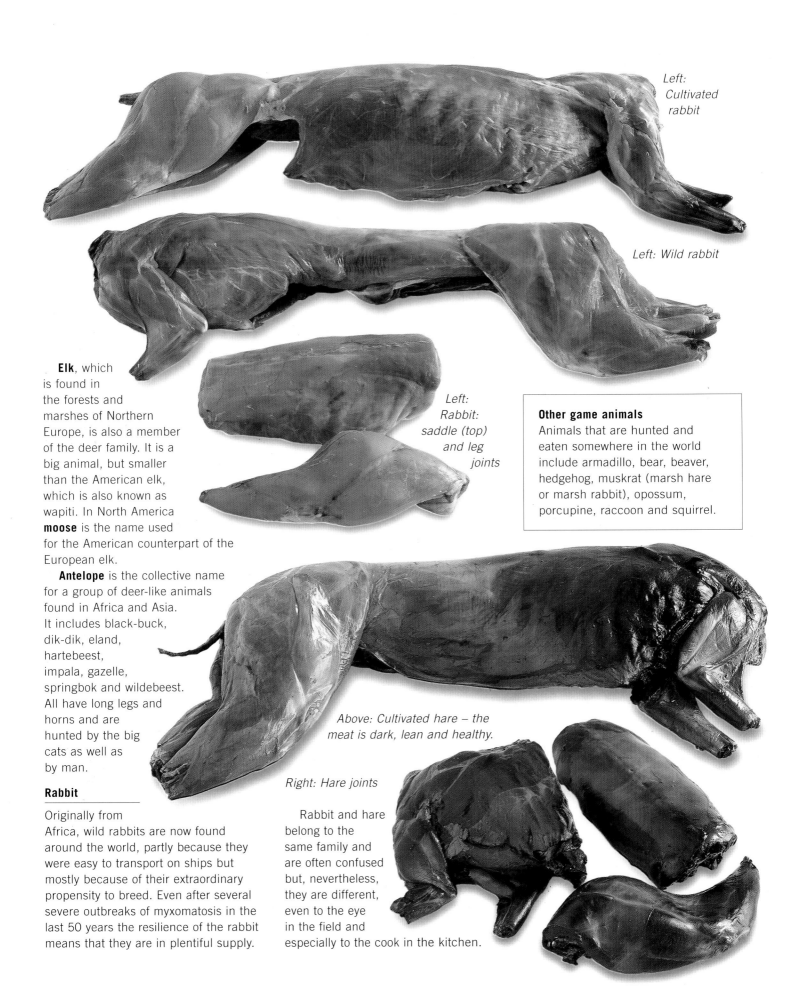

Left: Cultivated rabbit

Left: Wild rabbit

Left: Rabbit: saddle (top) and leg joints

Elk, which is found in the forests and marshes of Northern Europe, is also a member of the deer family. It is a big animal, but smaller than the American elk, which is also known as wapiti. In North America **moose** is the name used for the American counterpart of the European elk.

Antelope is the collective name for a group of deer-like animals found in Africa and Asia. It includes black-buck, dik-dik, eland, hartebeest, impala, gazelle, springbok and wildebeest. All have long legs and horns and are hunted by the big cats as well as by man.

Rabbit

Originally from Africa, wild rabbits are now found around the world, partly because they were easy to transport on ships but mostly because of their extraordinary propensity to breed. Even after several severe outbreaks of myxomatosis in the last 50 years the resilience of the rabbit means that they are in plentiful supply.

Other game animals
Animals that are hunted and eaten somewhere in the world include armadillo, bear, beaver, hedgehog, muskrat (marsh hare or marsh rabbit), opossum, porcupine, raccoon and squirrel.

Above: Cultivated hare – the meat is dark, lean and healthy.

Right: Hare joints

Rabbit and hare belong to the same family and are often confused but, nevertheless, they are different, even to the eye in the field and especially to the cook in the kitchen.

Rabbit is smaller and its flesh is pale and mild in flavour while hare is larger and its meat is dark and often very strong. Wild rabbit is usually bought whole and fresh, with or without its offal (innards), while tame rabbit can also be bought jointed. Frozen rabbit can also be obtained through imports mainly from China. The meat of the doe rabbit (the female) is more tender than that of the buck (the male).

Hare

Originally from Europe, hares are also now found around the world. They are larger than rabbits with longer ears and a notched – or hare – lip and powerful hind legs. The meat is dark and lean and healthy, and (in a young animal) very tender. Its flavour is stronger than rabbit. Hare can be roasted whole or jointed and used in casseroles, stews and terrines. Older hares are usually jugged (which is when it is cooked in a jug or deep earthenware casserole, set in a pan of water, either on the hob (stovetop) or in the oven). The water bath tempers the heat and ensures that the meat is cooked very gently and very slowly. Many traditional French dishes call for the back or saddle (*râble*) or the saddle and hind legs (*train*) only. The classic Tuscan dish using hare is *Pappardelle al Lepre*.

Wild boar

Found across Europe, Central Asia and North Africa, wild boar has been hunted for so many years it has attained a legendary cultural status. It was hunted to extinction in Britain in the 17th century but is still found in fairly large numbers – and still hunted enthusiastically – in Europe. The meat of wild boar has a strong taste. It is dark-coloured and, because there is little fat, can be dry and tough, although its flavour is excellent. For this reason it is usually marinated. Wild boar should be cooked in the same way as pork. Joints that are to be roasted should be larded with pork fat before cooking.

Above: Wild hare – these animals are now found all over the world, although they are originally from Europe.

Wines to serve with furred game

Big reds or port are the traditional wines to serve with game. Try a Barolo with venison; a New World Cabernet Sauvignon from California, Australia or Chile; Pinotage from South Africa or a Shiraz from Australia. Pinot Noirs, particularly those from America, are very good with venison cooked in red wine.

Try a fruity, intense red such as Spanish Rioja for rabbit cooked in red wine, a dry, oaked white such as Rioja Blanco for rabbit cooked in white wine, and a medium white such as South African Chenin Blanc with rabbit cooked in (hard) cider.

Left, clockwise from left: Wild boar saddle, fillet and chops, which can be treated like free-range pork.

PREPARING FURRED GAME

Furred game is sold hung and skinned, ready for cooking. When the meat is first slaughtered it is tough and lacks flavour; hanging helps it to become tender and to develop its flavour. If you shoot furred game, your local specialist may hang and skin the animal for you.

Jointing a rabbit or hare

Rabbits can be roasted whole, but are more usually jointed and then cooked slowly in casseroles and stews.

1 Cut the hind legs off the body, then cut between the hind legs.

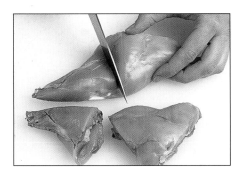

2 Cut each hind leg into two pieces.

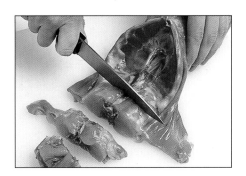

3 Cut the body into four pieces, then cut the rib section in half through the breastbone and backbone.

COOKING FURRED GAME

This is nowhere near as difficult as some people think. Approach venison in much the same way as you would a piece of beef. Wild boar is no more difficult than a piece of free-range pork. Tame rabbit can be compared with chicken, while wild rabbit simply needs patient casseroling. The secret with game is to roast young game and to braise, stew or casserole older and tougher animals. A good compromise between roasting and braising is to sauté the game, thereby using a moist rather than a dry heat to cook the meat.

Roasting venison

Prime cuts of venison, such as haunch, loin or best end, are juicy and tender when they are larded with fat, then roasted and served rare.

1 Venison is such a lean meat it helps to lard the joint before you roast it. Simply thread thin strips of pork fat through the outside of the meat using a larding needle.

2 Put the prepared joint on a roasting rack, standing in a large roasting pan, and brush the joint all over with a little olive oil or melted butter to help keep it moist during cooking.

3 Place the joint in an oven preheated to 190°C/375°F/Gas 5. The cooking time depends on the thickness and the size of the joint, but, generally, venison needs 15 minutes per 450g/1lb. Baste during cooking. Once cooked, allow the joint to stand for 10 minutes to make it easier to carve.

Carving a leg of venison

1 Hold the leg firmly by the shank with one hand, rounded muscle up. Cut a couple of slices lengthways to give the meat a base to sit on.

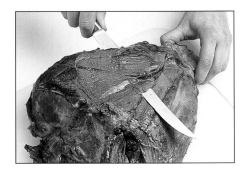

2 Turn the meat over, place it on a board and cut horizontal slices until you reach the bone. Turn the meat over and cut slices from the first side.

3 Cut short, thin slices from the meat remaining at the sides of the joint.

Roasting rabbit

Rabbit is generally tender enough to roast – particularly the saddle joint or saddle and hind legs.

1 Ensure that your roasting pan is large enough to hold the whole joint.

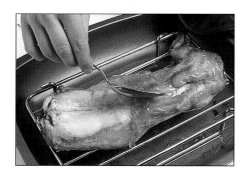

2 Place the rabbit on a rack in the roasting pan and brush the rabbit with olive oil or melted butter. Place the joint in the oven, preheated to 190°C/375°F/Gas 5 and cook for 20–30 minutes, until tender. Baste with the fat several times during cooking to keep it moist.

Marinades for furred game
Tough and dry cuts of furred game, such as venison, hare and wild boar, can greatly benefit from a flavoursome marinade. Leave the game to marinate overnight in one of the following combinations.
• Red wine with 2 chopped onions, 6 peppercorns, parsley, 1 bay leaf and 3 blades of mace.
• Red wine with 30ml/2 tbsp vegetable oil, 1 chopped onion, 1 chopped garlic clove, 2 bay leaves, 2–3 juniper berries and the pared rind of a lemon.

Marinating and grilling rabbit

This is a quick and easy way of cooking well-marinated pieces of rabbit. The close contact with the intense heat seals the meat quickly, thus sealing in all the juices, so you end up with a very flavourful and succulent piece of meat.

1 Put the rabbit joints in a non-metallic dish with sliced carrot and celery, 150ml/¼ pint/⅔ cup white wine and 50ml/2fl oz/¼ cup vegetable oil. Leave in the refrigerator to marinate overnight.

2 Place the rabbit joints on a lightly oiled grill (broiler) rack.

3 Cook the rabbit portions under a very hot, preheated grill for 2–3 minutes on each side, turning once, and brushing with a little extra oil halfway through the cooking time.

Pan-frying furred game

This is a quick way of cooking fillets of rabbit, venison loin chops or escalopes (US scallops) of wild boar. Use a non-stick, heavy pan.

1 Dab a little sunflower oil on kitchen paper and wipe out the inside of the frying pan. Heat the frying pan until it is very hot before adding the meat.

2 Cook for 2–3 minutes on each side, turning once with tongs.

Casseroling and pot-roasting

Venison cuts such as neck, shoulder and shin are often marinated and then casseroled because they benefit from long, gentle cooking. Rabbit pieces are also excellent in casseroles.

Brown the meat, then add the rest of the ingredients and simmer until tender.

Accompaniments for furred game
Game is served with the same accompaniments today as it was six or seven hundred years ago. Venison is served with redcurrant jelly, while rabbit is stewed with mushrooms and onions.

NEW MEATS

Beef, lamb, pork, chicken, turkey, duck and goose are long established as international meats, but there is also a wide selection of other types that have, until comparatively recently, rarely been sampled away from their countries of origin. Modern farming, rearing, butchering, food transportation, communications and marketing have fuelled interest in different culinary cultures. Unlike exotic fruit and vegetables, which tend to look and smell appetizing, many of the animal food sources have less visual appeal and they rarely sound exciting. These meats may not have the same impact as aromatic fruit or brightly coloured vegetables, but they are steadily gaining acceptance and arousing the interest of enthusiastic cooks.

Buying and storing

When they are available from the supermarket, the majority of these meats are neatly prepared ready for cooking, and displayed in sealed packs. Labelling information includes a date by which the product should be used and, often, instructions or ideas for basic cooking methods. Always treat them as you would other fresh meat, by storing the sealed pack in a dish in the coldest area of the refrigerator. Specialist butchers offer a wider selection of cuts, and they will also be able to offer advice on which cuts to buy and on cooking methods, too. Some new meats have been frozen and are sold thawed. Do not re-freeze previously frozen meats.

TYPES OF NEW MEAT

Alligator

There is a long tradition of cooking alligator in the southern states of America, particularly Louisiana. Fears of extinction meant that alligators in the wild were protected and so farmed alligator were introduced. Alligators are farmed (and

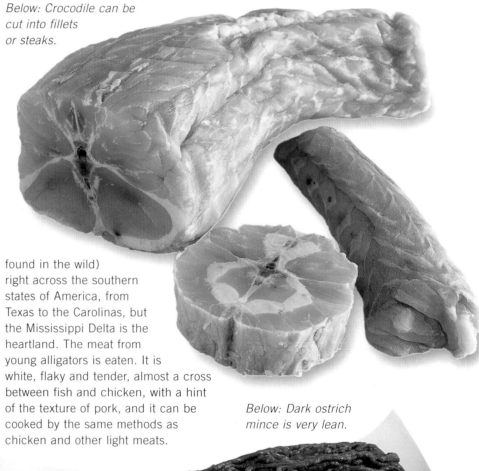

Above: Alligator steaks have a flaky texture.

Below: Crocodile can be cut into fillets or steaks.

found in the wild) right across the southern states of America, from Texas to the Carolinas, but the Mississippi Delta is the heartland. The meat from young alligators is eaten. It is white, flaky and tender, almost a cross between fish and chicken, with a hint of the texture of pork, and it can be cooked by the same methods as chicken and other light meats.

Crocodile

Larger than alligators, crocodiles are found in the northern part of the Nile Delta, the swamps of Florida and Asia, from Australia and the Philippines right across to southern India. The meat is popular in the Northern Territory of Australia where both freshwater and marine species are farmed. Like alligator, crocodile is a tender meat with a delicate flavour, similar to chicken or pork, but it has a slightly flaky texture. Crocodile is available as steaks or fillets, and is cooked as for chicken.

Below: Dark ostrich mince is very lean.

Ostrich

This bird is native to Africa, where it has been eaten since prehistoric times. It is now farmed in North America and Western Europe. Ostrich meat is dark in colour and finer in texture than beef. It is a lean meat with a full flavour, stronger than beef but not quite as pronounced as game, and is sold as prepared cuts, including slices, steaks, fillet and mince (ground). Prepare and cook by grilling (broiling), pan-frying, stir-frying, roasting or braising. Minced ostrich can be used instead of beef for burgers, meatloaves and sauces.

Emu

Indigenous to Australia, where it is farmed as well as being found in the wild. Emu meat is dark and lean. It is darker than beef but has a softer texture. Emu should be cooked in the same way as tender beef. It is also smoked and sold as a cured meat; and used for making sausages. Cuts include fillet, steaks, cubed meat and mince. Emu can be grilled, roasted, pan-fried or braised.

Below: Emu steak

Kangaroo

This is a generic name applied to different Australian species, including large red and small grey kangaroos, wallaroos and wallabies. Kangaroo has long been a traditional part of the Aborigine diet and is now internationally available. It is a dark, fine-textured meat with a strong flavour, more pronounced than beef; it has been compared to hare, but depending on the cooking method, kangaroo meat is not necessarily that rich. Sold as prepared cuts, including steaks and slices, kangaroo is also available as a smoked meat. In terms of cooking, it is best treated as beef. Forerib, sirloin or fillet cuts are sold for roasting; while rump, sirloin or fillet are suitable for frying or grilling. Kangaroo is a good ingredient for slow-cooked casseroles and stews.

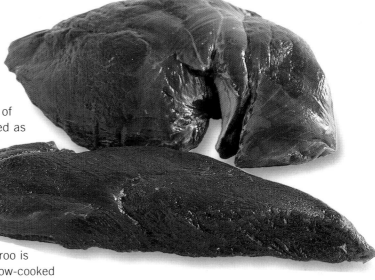

Above: Large cuts of kangaroo can be roasted like beef, while steaks are often grilled or pan-fried.

Above: Ostrich fillet and steak have a rich, gamey flavour.

Buffalo

The Cape buffalo is hunted and eaten in Africa, and air-dried and smoked to make biltong. The river buffalo and the swamp buffalo are found in Asia and in North America there is the bison. Buffalo meat is similar to beef, with cuts that can be roasted, grilled, fried, stewed or braised.

Llama

In South America, the llama has long provided transport, clothing and a source of milk and meat, particularly among the Peruvians. To modern tastes, younger llamas are more tender and appetizing than older beasts (the meat of which is more usually dried and turned into *charqui* or jerky). Roast a joint or leg of llama; pan-fry, griddle or barbecue cutlets or loin chops.

Below: Buffalo is similar to beef and has corresponding cuts, like this rolled and tied joint, which can be roasted.

COOKING NEW MEATS

Smaller cuts can all be cooked quickly by dry methods such as grilling (broiling), pan-frying and griddling. Roast larger joints following timings for beef.

Pan-frying buffalo

Buffalo steak should be treated in the same way as beef steak. Trim off excess fat, and beat out the meat with a meat mallet to ensure that it is evenly thick.

Grease a frying pan very lightly with oil and heat it well. Add the steak to the pan and cook over a high heat until it is browned on both sides. For a well-cooked steak, reduce the heat slightly and continue cooking until the meat is cooked through to your liking.

Pan-frying kangaroo

Tender steaks from the fillet, rump or sirloin can be pan-fried as for beef.

Grease a frying pan with a little oil and heat it until hot before adding the meat. Cook over a high heat until browned on one side, then turn and cook the second side. Kangaroo steaks can be served rare, medium or well cooked. For a well-cooked steak, reduce the heat slightly once the meat is browned and cook until cooked right through.

Pan-frying emu

Tender emu steak should be cut evenly, 2–5cm/¾–2in thick.

Heat a little oil in a frying pan, then add the meat when the oil is very hot. Cook for 1–2 minutes on each side, until well browned and just cooked through. Do not overcook the steak. Add salt and pepper to taste and serve at once.

Preparing ostrich stir-fry

1 Lay the ostrich steak between two sheets of baking parchment and beat it out evenly with a meat mallet. Cut the thinned steak into fine strips.

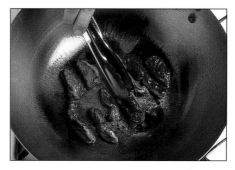

2 Heat a wok, then add a little oil. When very hot, add the ostrich strips and cook over a high heat for 30–60 seconds, stirring or turning frequently until the strips are evenly browned.

3 Use a slotted spoon to remove the meat from the pan and set it aside. Cook the vegetables for the stir-fry and replace the meat for 1–2 minutes before adding a sauce and serving.

Preparing and sealing diced ostrich

Ostrich (and emu) are good casseroled or braised.

1 Cut the ostrich steak into strips, then across into even-size cubes.

2 Heat a little oil in a frying pan. Add the cubed meat and cook, turning occasionally, until browned on all sides. Use a slotted spoon to remove the meat from the pan, then continue preparing the casserole and sauce. Return the ostrich to the pan for 5–10 minutes more to gently reheat the meat. Take care not to overcook it.

Griddling ostrich

This is an excellent method for ostrich meat, which is best served still rare or medium in the middle.

Heat the griddle until very hot, then add a little vegetable oil and heat again. Lay the ostrich steaks on the griddle and cook for 1–2 minutes on each side. Serve at once.

Grilling ostrich

Similar, speedy cooking is essential when grilling (broiling) ostrich steaks.

Thoroughly preheat the grill (broiler). Lay the meat on a grill rack and brush lightly with oil, then season with ground black pepper. Cook for no more than 2 minutes on each side, until browned outside but moist in the middle. Top with a knob of herb and lemon butter and serve at once.

Grilling crocodile steaks

1 Preheat the grill to high. Select evenly thick crocodile steaks and lay them on a grill rack. Brush them with a little oil or a basting sauce.

2 Place at a medium distance from the grill and cook until well browned. Turn and brush with more oil or sauce.

3 Cook until well browned on the other side. Test the centre of the steak with the point of a knife to check that the meat is cooked through: it should be firm and flake easily. If the meat is soft and not fully cooked, reduce the heat slightly and continue grilling the steak.

Cooking alligator or crocodile in a rich cream sauce

1 Melt a knob of butter in a little oil in a frying pan. When foaming, add small portions of alligator or crocodile fillet.

2 Cook over a high heat until browned on one side, then turn and brown the second side until the pieces are firm and just cooked through.

3 Grate a little lime rind over the meat and season well with salt and ground black pepper.

4 Add a splash of dry white wine, then pour in some double (heavy) cream and cook until the cream is just below simmering point. Stir occasionally to move the pieces of meat around in the sauce. Taste for seasoning and sprinkle with chopped parsley. Serve at once.

Baking crocodile fillet en papillote

1 Season the fillet and rub it all over with the chosen flavouring ingredients. Here finely chopped garlic and chillies are used. Cut the fillet into neat, even-size portions.

2 Wrap each portion of meat in a piece of baking parchment. Fold the edges of the paper together and tuck the ends under to seal. Place the packages in a roasting pan and cook in the oven at 200°C/400°F/Gas 6 for 20 minutes, or until fully cooked.

STOCKS AND SAUCES

We use the word stock simply because it was something most cooks kept a stock of for use in the kitchen. These days, sadly, it tends to mean something you get when you add a kettleful of boiling water to a stock cube (or a bouillon cube as it is called in the United States and France).

Traditionally, stock was the product of a pot kept simmering on the hob (stovetop) to which leftovers, such as pieces of poultry and game as well as bones, vegetables, vegetable trimmings and herbs, were added. The cook then always had a stock of broth, packed with flavour, to use as a basis for soups, stews and sauces. These days few households have a stockpot on the go and small batches are usually made as and when required. Nevertheless, a good, home-made stock has much more flavour than a cube and it is well worth making your own.

A well-flavoured stock is the basis of good cooking – which is why young chefs are always judged by the quality of the stocks they make – and if a stock is poor then the resulting soups, casseroles, sauces and gravies coming out of the restaurant kitchen will be poor, too. That's why, although stocks are not difficult to make, professional chefs spend so long getting them right.

There are, basically, two different types of stock: a brown stock in which the bones are browned in the oven first, and a white stock in which the bones are poached rather than roasted. Brown stocks are normally made from dark meats such as venison and are used for making consommés, soups, and dark sauces and for cooking with dark meats. White stocks are made from chicken and turkey bones and are used for making soups, white sauces and for cooking with white meats.

The reason people go wrong when making stock is that they think it's just a pot for leftovers. It was, historically, but the way to get a really good stock is to use fresh bones and vegetables. Never add salt to a stock until the end of cooking and always use whole peppercorns because ground pepper will only make the stock taste bitter.

White poultry stock

MAKES ABOUT 1 LITRE/1¾ PINTS/4 CUPS

INGREDIENTS
    1 fresh or cooked poultry carcass
    1 large onion, quartered
    1 celery stick, sliced
    1 carrot, thickly sliced
    6 peppercorns
    bouquet garni

1 Using poultry shears, chop the carcass into pieces and put in a large pan. Cover with water.

2 Add the vegetables, peppercorns and bouquet garni to the pan and bring slowly to the boil.

3 Using a slotted spoon, skim well, removing as much scum as possible, and simmer gently for 2–3 hours.

4 Strain through a sieve, then gently press the bones and vegetables to extract as much flavour as possible (but don't push so hard that the vegetables start to go into the stock).

5 Leave the liquid to cool completely, then chill it overnight (the fat will rise to the top, then solidify, when it can easily be removed).

6 If you don't have time to let the stock cool, skim off as much fat as possible with a spoon and then carefully draw absorbent kitchen paper across the top of the stock to remove the surface fat. Store in the refrigerator and boil up every day or freeze.

Brown poultry stock

MAKES ABOUT 1 LITRE/1¾ PINTS/4 CUPS

INGREDIENTS
    1 fresh or cooked poultry carcass
       with giblets but not the liver
    1 tbsp sunflower oil
    1 onion, sliced
    1 carrot, sliced
    450ml/¾ pint/scant 2 cups water
    2 sprigs parsley
    1 bay leaf
    1 sprig fresh thyme

1 Chop the carcass into pieces. Heat the oil in a large pan or stock pot, add the carcass pieces and cook until browned, stirring frequently.

2 Add the vegetables, liquid and herbs and simmer for 1½ hours, skimming if necessary. Strain through a sieve, pressing to extract the flavour. Leave the liquid to cool, then chill overnight. Remove any fat that has solidified.

White sauce

This classic basic roux-based milk sauce is excellent for white meats, such as chicken and other types of poultry, but is also good with new meats like alligator and crocodile.

MAKES ABOUT 600ML/1 PINT/2½ CUPS

INGREDIENTS
  50g/2oz/¼ cup butter
  30ml/2 tbsp plain (all-purpose) flour
  600ml/1 pint/2½ cups milk
  salt and ground pepper

1 Melt the butter in a small pan.

2 Add the flour and cook for 1 minute, stirring all the time.

3 Turn off the heat and gradually stir in the milk.

4 Return the pan to the heat, bring the sauce to the boil, stirring all the time.

5 Simmer for 1 minute and season. This makes a coating sauce. To make a thin, pouring sauce, add another 300ml/ ½ pint/1¼ cups milk.

Béchamel sauce

Follow the recipe for white sauce but add 1 quartered onion, 1 sliced carrot, 1 sliced celery stick, 1 bay leaf and 6 peppercorns to the milk. Bring to the boil, infuse for 30 minutes, then strain.

Parsley sauce

This is the traditional sauce to serve with poached chicken.

Follow the recipe for white sauce and add 30ml/2 tbsp finely chopped parsley with the salt and pepper.

Mushroom sauce

This is a perfect accompaniment for buffalo and ostrich steaks.

Follow the recipe for white sauce but first, pan-fry 115g/4oz/1⅔ cups sliced mushrooms, such as shiitake, and 1 finely chopped garlic clove. Stir the mushroom mixture into the white sauce.

Cranberry sauce

This is the traditional accompaniment for roast turkey.

MAKES ABOUT 600ML/1 PINT/2½ CUPS

INGREDIENTS
  350g/12oz/3 cups fresh or
    frozen cranberries
  175g/6oz/scant 1 cup golden
    caster (superfine) sugar
  15ml/1 tbsp Cointreau
  1.5ml/¼ tsp mixed (apple pie) spice
  ground black pepper
  grated rind 2 oranges
  50ml/2fl oz/¼ cup orange juice

Put all the ingredients in a large heavy pan. Cook gently over a low heat until the sugar is completely dissolved. Bring to the boil, then reduce the heat slightly and simmer, stirring occasionally, for 20–25 minutes, or until thickened.

Tomato sauce

This slightly spicy sauce is delicious with poultry and game, and alligator.

MAKES ABOUT 1.2 LITRES/2 PINTS/5 CUPS

INGREDIENTS
    900g/2lb ripe tomatoes, quartered
    225g/8oz onions
    450g/1lb cooking apples, peeled
        and cored
    1.2 litres/2 pints/5 cups distilled
        white vinegar
    25g/1oz mustard seeds, crushed
    1 dried chilli
    5cm/2in piece cinnamon stick
    3 blades of mace
    6 peppercorns
    2.5ml/½ tsp grated nutmeg
    50g/2oz/¼ cup sea salt
    225g/8oz/generous 1 cup golden
        granulated sugar

1 Put the tomatoes in a preserving pan. Finely chop the onions and apples, and add to the pan with half the vinegar. Stir in the spices, flavourings and salt, and stir well. Bring the mixture slowly to the boil and simmer for 1–1½ hours, or until reduced by about one-third.

2 Sieve the pulp. Return the mixture to the pan with the remaining vinegar and all of the sugar and stir over a gentle heat until the sugar has dissolved. Bring to the boil and simmer for 30 minutes, or until the sauce has thickened. Pour into sterilized, warmed bottles and seal. Store in the refrigerator for 1 week.

Orange sauce

A tangy sauce for roast duck and game.

MAKES ABOUT 450ML/¾ PINT/2 CUPS

INGREDIENTS
    25g/1oz/2 tbsp butter
    40g/1½oz/⅓ cup plain (all-purpose) flour
    300ml/½ pint/1¼ cups poultry stock
    150ml/¼ pint/⅔ cup red wine
    2 oranges
    10ml/2 tsp lemon juice
    15ml/1 tbsp orange-flavoured liqueur
    30ml/2 tbsp redcurrant jelly
    salt and ground black pepper

1 Melt the butter in a small pan over a medium heat. Add the flour and cook for about 3 minutes, stirring all the time, until lightly browned.

2 Without heating, gradually stir in the stock and red wine. Bring to the boil, stirring, then simmer for 5 minutes.

3 Thinly peel the orange rind from one of the oranges using a swivel-bladed peeler. Put the rind in a pan, cover with cold water and bring to the boil. Cook for 5 minutes, then drain.

4 Meanwhile, squeeze the juice from both oranges into the sauce. Add the lemon juice, orange-flavoured liqueur and orange rind, with the redcurrant jelly. Stir the sauce, then reheat gently. Season to taste with salt and pepper before serving.

Bread sauce

Perfect for poultry and game birds.

MAKES ABOUT 450ML/¾ PINT/2 CUPS

INGREDIENTS
    1 onion
    6 cloves
    1 bay leaf
    300ml/½ pint/1¼ cups milk
    150ml/¼ pint/⅔ cup single
        (light) cream
    115g/4oz/2 cups fresh white
        breadcrumbs
    knob of butter
    salt and ground black pepper

1 Stud the onion with the cloves. Put the onion, bay leaf and milk in a pan and bring slowly to the boil. Remove from the heat and leave to stand for at least 30 minutes to allow the flavour of the onion to infuse into the milk.

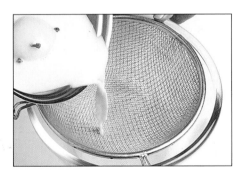

2 Strain the milk and discard the clove-studded onion and the bay leaf.

3 Pour the milk into a clean pan and add the single cream and breadcrumbs. Bring slowly to the boil, then reduce the heat and simmer gently for 5 minutes. Stir in the butter and season with salt and pepper to taste just before serving.

GRAVIES

The classic gravies, served with meat dishes by Auguste Escoffier at the Savoy and the Ritz Carlton in the 1890s, are a world away from the gravy that comes by adding boiling water to stock cubes or freeze-dried gravy granules. The traditional British meat gravy – which ranges in colour from pale gold to dark brown – is made with what is left in the bottom of the pan after a joint has been roasted, deglazed with good stock and carefully seasoned. Some gravies are quite thick, others rather thin; it is really a matter of personal preference. Many cooks add a spoonful of flour to help thicken the gravy although purists condemn the practice.

In France, *jus de viande* is a version of a thin British gravy. Red eye gravy, famous in the American south for being served with ham and other pork dishes, is made by adding a little water (or, sometimes, strong black coffee) to the roasting pan and simmering it until it bubbles and turns red. Another version adds a teaspoon of brown sugar, stirred in until it caramelizes, before the water is added.

Thickened gravy

This classic gravy is perfect to serve with all roast meats and poultry.

MAKES ABOUT 450ML/¾ PINT/2 CUPS

INGREDIENTS
  25g/1oz/¼ cup plain (all-purpose) flour
  450ml/¾ pint/scant 2 cups good-quality stock
  45ml/3 tbsp port or sherry
  salt and ground black pepper

1 Tilt the roasting pan and spoon off almost all the fat, leaving the meat juices behind.

2 Sprinkle the flour into the pan and heat gently for 1 minute, stirring all the time. Gradually add the stock, stirring constantly until thickened. Add the port or sherry, season with salt and pepper and simmer gently for 1–2 minutes more. Taste and adjust the seasoning, if necessary. Serve piping hot.

Onion gravy

This is the ideal gravy to serve with fried and grilled steaks.

MAKES ABOUT 450ML/¾ PINT/2 CUPS

INGREDIENTS
  30ml/2 tbsp olive oil
  25g/1oz/2 tbsp butter
  8 onions, sliced
  5ml/1 tsp caster (superfine) sugar
  15ml/1 tbsp plain (all-purpose) flour
  300ml/½ pint/1¼ cups brown
    meat stock
  salt and ground black pepper

1 Heat the oil and butter in a pan until foaming, then add the onions. Mix well, so the onions are coated in the butter mixture. Cover the pan and cook gently for 30 minutes, stirring frequently. Add the caster sugar and cook for a further 5 minutes; the onions will soften, caramelize and reduce.

2 Turn off the heat and stir in the flour.

3 Gradually add the stock and return the pan to the heat. Bring the onion gravy to the boil, stirring all the time.

4 Simmer for 2–3 minutes or until thickened, then season with salt and pepper to taste.

A glaze is used to give a dish an especially smooth, shiny (and sometimes transparent) finish. A meat glaze is made through the prolonged reduction of meat stock, resulting in a syrupy liquid. Alcohol, such as Madeira, is often added to the reduction and a little butter, whisked in at the end, to give a smooth, satiny appearance.

POULTRY DISHES

Chickens and poussins, turkeys, ducks, geese and guinea fowl are domesticated birds, specially reared for the pot. They are at their best cooked simply, and all make delicious and healthy meals. This section opens with a classic recipe for Roast Chicken with Madeira Gravy and Bread Sauce and includes the quintessential French dish Coq au Vin, but there are also light, summery recipes such as Chicken and Asparagus Risotto, and Chicken with Tarragon Cream. Guinea Fowl is cooked with a creamy whisky sauce, while duck is prepared in a fresh, tart plum sauce, and there are salads, too — the most spectacular, a divine recipe that combines lightly dressed leaves with poached eggs and skewers of crisply cooked duck.

ROAST CHICKEN WITH MADEIRA GRAVY AND BREAD SAUCE

THIS IS A SIMPLE, TRADITIONAL DISH WHICH TASTES WONDERFUL AND MAKES A PERFECT FAMILY MEAL. ROAST POTATOES AND SEASONAL GREEN VEGETABLES, SUCH AS BRUSSELS SPROUTS STIR-FRIED WITH CHESTNUTS, ARE DELICIOUS WITH ROAST CHICKEN.

SERVES FOUR

INGREDIENTS
   50g/2oz/¼ cup butter
   1 onion, chopped
   75g/3oz/1½ cups fresh white
     breadcrumbs
   grated rind of 1 lemon
   30ml/2 tbsp chopped fresh parsley
   30ml/2 tbsp chopped fresh tarragon
   1 egg yolk
   1.5kg/3¼lb oven-ready chicken
   175g/6oz rindless streaky (fatty)
     bacon rashers (strips)
   salt and ground black pepper
For the bread sauce
   1 onion, studded with 6 cloves
   1 bay leaf
   300ml/½ pint/1¼ cups milk
   150ml/¼ pint/⅔ cup single
     (light) cream
   115g/4oz/2 cups fresh white
     breadcrumbs
   knob of butter
For the gravy
   10ml/2 tsp plain (all-purpose) flour
   300ml/½ pint/1¼ cups well-
     flavoured chicken stock
   dash of Madeira or sherry

1 Preheat the oven to 200°C/400°F/ Gas 6. First make the stuffing. Melt half the butter in a pan and fry the onion for about 5 minutes, or until softened.

2 Remove the pan from the heat and add the breadcrumbs, lemon rind, parsley and half the chopped tarragon. Season with salt and pepper, then mix in the egg yolk to bind the ingredients into a moist stuffing.

VARIATION
Cocktail sausages, which have been wrapped in thin streaky bacon rashers make a delicious accompaniment to roast chicken. Roast them alongside the chicken for the final 25–30 minutes cooking time.

3 Fill the neck end of the chicken with stuffing, then truss the chicken neatly and weigh it. To calculate the cooking time, allow 20 minutes per 450g/1lb, plus 20 minutes.

4 Put the chicken in a roasting pan and season it well with salt and pepper. Beat together the remaining butter and tarragon, then smear this over the bird.

5 Lay the bacon rashers over the top of the chicken (this helps stop the light breast meat from drying out) and roast for the calculated time. Baste the bird every 30 minutes during cooking and cover with buttered foil if the bacon begins to overbrown.

6 Meanwhile, make the bread sauce. Put the clove-studded onion, bay leaf and milk in a small, heavy pan and bring slowly to the boil. Remove the pan from the heat and leave the milk to stand for at least 30 minutes so that it is gently infused with the flavouring ingredients.

7 Strain the milk into a clean pan (discard the flavouring ingredients) and add the cream and breadcrumbs. Bring slowly to the boil, stirring continuously, then reduce the heat and simmer gently for 5 minutes. Keep warm while you make the gravy and carve the chicken, then stir in the butter and season to taste just before serving.

8 Transfer the chicken to a warmed serving dish, cover tightly with foil and leave to stand for 10 minutes.

9 To make the gravy, pour off all but 15ml/1 tbsp fat from the roasting pan. Place the pan on the hob (stovetop) and stir in the flour. Cook the flour for 1 minute, or until golden brown, then stir in the stock and Madeira or sherry. Bring to the boil, stirring all the time, then simmer for about 3 minutes until thickened. Add seasoning to taste and strain the gravy into a warm sauceboat.

10 Carve the chicken and serve it at once, with the stuffing, gravy and hot bread sauce.

COOK'S TIP
To keep chicken moist during roasting, some recipes suggest cooking the bird on its sides, turning it halfway through cooking, and others place the breast down. Covering the top of the chicken breast with rashers of bacon and adding foil to prevent this from overcooking is the easiest and most effective method.

ESCALOPES OF CHICKEN WITH BABY VEGETABLES

THIS IS A QUICK AND LIGHT DISH — IDEAL FOR SUMMER, WHEN IT IS TOO HOT TO SLAVE OVER THE STOVE FOR HOURS OR TO EAT HEAVY MEALS. FLATTENING THE CHICKEN BREASTS THINS THE MEAT AND ALSO SPEEDS UP THE COOKING.

2 Heat 45ml/3 tbsp of the oil in a frying pan and cook the chicken escalopes (US scallops) for 10 minutes on each side, turning frequently.

3 Meanwhile, put the baby potatoes and carrots in a pan with the remaining oil and season with sea salt. Cover and cook over a medium heat for a further 10–15 minutes, stirring frequently. Add the fennel and cook for 5 minutes more, stirring frequently. Finally, add the peas and asparagus and cook for 5 minutes more, or until all the vegetables are cooked and tender.

4 To make the sauce, mix together the mayonnaise and sun-dried tomato paste in a small bowl. Spoon the vegetables on to a warmed large serving platter or individual plates and place the chicken on top. Serve the tomato mayonnaise either separately or with the chicken and vegetables. Garnish with a few sprigs of flat leaf parsley.

COOK'S TIP
Any combinations of baby vegetables can be used. The weight is for prepared vegetables (they are usually sold trimmed). Adjust the cooking time or the order in which they are added to the pan according to how long the chosen vegetables take to cook, for example add root vegetables first, before quick-cooking courgettes (zucchini), French (green) beans, mangetouts or similar delicate ingredients.

SERVES FOUR

INGREDIENTS
    4 skinless, boneless chicken breast
        portions, each weighing 175g/6oz
    juice of 1 lime
    120ml/4fl oz/½ cup olive oil
    675g/1½lb mixed baby potatoes,
        carrots, fennel (sliced if large),
        peas and asparagus
    sea salt and ground black pepper
    sprigs of fresh flat leaf parsley,
        to garnish
For the tomato mayonnaise
    150ml/¼ pint/⅔ cup mayonnaise
    15ml/1 tbsp sun-dried
        tomato paste

1 Lay the chicken breast portions between two sheets of clear film (plastic wrap) and use a rolling pin to beat them flat until they are evenly thin. Season the chicken with salt and pepper and sprinkle with the lime juice.

COQ <u>AU</u> VIN

THIS FRENCH COUNTRY CASSEROLE WAS TRADITIONALLY MADE WITH AN OLD BOILING BIRD, MARINATED OVERNIGHT IN RED WINE, THEN SIMMERED GENTLY UNTIL TENDER. MODERN RECIPES USE TENDER ROASTING BIRDS TO SAVE TIME AND BECAUSE BOILING FOWL ARE NOT READILY AVAILABLE.

SERVES SIX

INGREDIENTS
    45ml/3 tbsp light olive oil
    12 shallots
    225g/8oz rindless streaky (fatty)
      bacon rashers (strips), chopped
    3 garlic cloves, finely chopped
    225g/8oz small mushrooms, halved
    6 boneless chicken thighs
    3 boneless chicken breast portions
    1 bottle red wine
    salt and ground black pepper
    45ml/3 tbsp chopped fresh parsley,
      to garnish
For the bouquet garni
    3 sprigs each of fresh parsley, thyme
      and sage
    1 bay leaf
    4 peppercorns
For the beurre manié
    25g/1oz/2 tbsp butter, softened
    25g/1oz/¼ cup plain (all-purpose) flour

1 Heat the oil in a large, flameproof casserole, add the shallots and cook for 5 minutes, or until golden. Increase the heat, add the bacon, garlic and halved mushrooms and cook for 10 minutes more, stirring frequently.

2 Use a draining spoon to transfer the cooked ingredients to a plate. Halve the chicken breast portions, then brown, along with the thighs, in the oil remaining in the pan. As they cook, turn them to ensure they are golden brown all over. Return the shallots, garlic, mushrooms and bacon to the casserole and pour in the red wine.

3 Tie the ingredients for the bouquet garni in a bundle in a small piece of muslin and add to the casserole. Bring to the boil, reduce the heat and cover the casserole, then simmer for about 35 minutes.

4 To make the beurre manié, cream the butter and flour together in a small bowl using your fingers or a spoon to make a smooth paste.

5 Add small lumps of this paste to the bubbling casserole, stirring well until each piece has melted into the liquid before adding the next. When all the paste has been added, bring back to the boil and simmer for 5 minutes.

6 Season the casserole to taste with salt and pepper and serve garnished with chopped fresh parsley and accompanied by boiled potatoes.

CHICKEN AND ASPARAGUS RISOTTO

USE THICK ASPARAGUS, IF POSSIBLE, AS FINE SPEARS OVERCOOK IN THIS RISOTTO. THE THICK ENDS OF THE ASPARAGUS ARE FULL OF FLAVOUR AND THEY BECOME BEAUTIFULLY TENDER IN THE TIME IT TAKES FOR THE RICE TO ABSORB THE STOCK.

SERVES FOUR

INGREDIENTS
  50g/2oz/¼ cup butter
  15ml/1 tbsp olive oil
  1 leek, finely chopped
  115g/4oz/1½ cups oyster
    mushrooms, sliced
  3 skinless, boneless chicken
    breast portions, cubed
  350g/12oz asparagus
  250g/9oz/1¼ cups risotto rice
  900ml/1½ pints/3¾ cups boiling
    chicken stock
  salt and ground black pepper
  Parmesan cheese curls, to serve

1 Heat the butter with the oil in a pan until the mixture is foaming. Add the leek and cook gently until softened, but not coloured. Add the mushrooms and cook for 5 minutes. Remove the vegetables from the pan and set aside.

2 Increase the heat and cook the cubes of chicken until golden on all sides. Do this in batches, if necessary, and then replace them all in the pan.

3 Meanwhile, discard the woody ends from the asparagus and cut the spears in half. Set the fine tips aside. Cut the thick ends in half and add to the pan. Return the leek and mushroom mixture to the pan and stir in the rice.

4 Pour in a ladleful of boiling stock and cook, stirring occasionally, until the stock is all absorbed. Continue adding the stock a ladleful at a time, simmering until it is absorbed, the rice is tender and the chicken is cooked.

COOK'S TIP
Use a cheese slicer or vegetable peeler to pare thin curls off a large piece of fresh Parmesan cheese.

5 Add the fine aspargus tips with the last ladleful of boiling stock for the final 5 minutes and continue cooking the risotto gently until the asparagus is tender. The whole process should take about 25–30 minutes.

6 Season the risotto to taste with salt and lots of ground black pepper and spoon it into individual warm serving bowls. Top each bowl with curls of Parmesan, and serve.

CHICKEN WITH TARRAGON CREAM

THE ANISEED-LIKE FLAVOUR OF TARRAGON HAS A PARTICULAR AFFINITY WITH CHICKEN, ESPECIALLY IN CREAMY SAUCES SUCH AS THE ONE IN THIS FAVOURITE FRENCH BISTRO-STYLE DISH. SERVE SEASONAL VEGETABLES AND BOILED RED CAMARGUE RICE WITH THE CHICKEN.

SERVES FOUR

INGREDIENTS

30ml/2 tbsp light olive oil
4 chicken supremes, each weighing
   about 250g/9oz
3 shallots, finely chopped
2 garlic cloves, finely chopped
115g/4oz/1½ cups wild mushrooms
   or shiitake mushrooms, halved
150ml/¼ pint/⅔ cup dry white wine
300ml/½ pint/1¼ cups double
   (heavy) cream
15g/½oz mixed fresh tarragon and
   flat leaf parsley, chopped
salt and ground black pepper
sprigs of fresh tarragon and flat leaf
   parsley, to garnish

COOK'S TIP
Wild mushrooms such as chanterelles or ceps are ideal.

1 Heat the light olive oil in a large frying pan and add the chicken supremes, skin-side down. Cook for 10 minutes, turning the chicken twice, or until it is a golden brown colour on both sides.

2 Reduce the heat and cook the chicken breasts for 10 minutes more, turning occasionally. Use a slotted spoon to remove the chicken breast portions from the pan and set aside.

3 Add the shallots and garlic to the pan and cook gently, stirring occasionally, until the shallots are softened but not browned. Increase the heat, add the mushrooms and stir-fry for 2 minutes, or until the mushrooms begin to colour.

4 Replace the chicken, nestling the pieces down into the other ingredients, and then pour in the wine. Simmer for 5–10 minutes, or until most of the wine has evaporated.

5 Add the cream and gently move the ingredients around in the pan to mix in the cream. Simmer for 10 minutes, or until the sauce has thickened. Stir the chopped herbs into the sauce with seasoning to taste. Arrange the chicken on warm plates and spoon the sauce over. Garnish with sprigs of tarragon and flat leaf parsley.

STUFFED CHICKEN IN BACON COATS

A SIMPLE CREAM CHEESE AND CHIVE FILLING FLAVOURS THESE CHICKEN BREASTS AND THEY ARE BEAUTIFULLY MOIST WHEN COOKED IN THEIR BACON WRAPPING. SERVE JACKET POTATOES AND A CRISP, FRESH GREEN SALAD AS ACCOMPANIMENTS.

SERVES FOUR

INGREDIENTS

   4 skinless, boneless chicken breast
     portions, each weighing 175g/6oz
   115g/4oz/½ cup cream cheese
   15ml/1 tbsp snipped chives
   8 rindless unsmoked bacon
     rashers (strips)
   15ml/1 tbsp olive oil
   ground black pepper

1 Preheat the oven to 200°C/400°F/ Gas 6. Using a sharp knife, make a horizontal slit from the side into each chicken breast portion (the cheese is stuffed into each slit).

2 To make the filling, beat together the cream cheese and chives. Divide the filling into four portions and, using a teaspoon, fill each slit with some of the cream cheese. Push the sides of the slit together to keep the filling in.

3 Wrap each breast in two rashers of bacon and place in an ovenproof dish. Drizzle the oil over the chicken and bake for 25–30 minutes, brushing occasionally with the oil. Season with black pepper and serve at once.

SOUTHERN FRIED CHICKEN

COLONEL SANDERS OPENED THE FIRST OF THOUSANDS OF "FINGER LICKIN' GOOD" KENTUCKY FRIED CHICKEN RESTAURANT FRANCHISES IN 1955, AFTER HIS OWN ROADSIDE RESTAURANT HAD TO CLOSE FOR LACK OF CUSTOM WHEN PASSING TRAFFIC WAS DIVERTED ON TO A NEW HIGHWAY. THIS IS A LOW-FAT INTERPRETATION OF THE ORIGINAL DEEP-FRIED DISH, WHICH IS NOW AN INTERNATIONAL FAST FOOD FAVOURITE. SERVE WITH POTATO WEDGES TO COMPLETE THE MEAL.

SERVES FOUR

INGREDIENTS

   15ml/1 tbsp paprika
   30ml/2 tbsp plain (all-purpose) flour
   4 skinless, boneless chicken breast
     portions, each weighing 175g/6oz
   30ml/2 tbsp sunflower oil
   salt and ground black pepper
For the corn cakes
   200g/7oz sweetcorn kernels
   350g/12oz mashed potato, cooled
   25g/1oz/2 tbsp butter
To serve
   150ml/¼ pint/⅔ cup sour cream
   15ml/1 tbsp snipped chives

COOK'S TIP

To make the mashed potato, cook the potatoes in boiling salted water for about 20 minutes until tender, then drain well. Add a little milk and mash until smooth.

1 Mix the paprika and flour together on a plate. Coat each chicken breast portion in the seasoned flour.

2 Heat the oil in a large frying pan and add the floured chicken. Cook over a high heat until a golden brown colour on both sides. Reduce the heat and continue cooking for 20 minutes more, turning once or twice, or until the chicken is cooked right through.

3 Meanwhile, make the corn cakes. Stir the sweetcorn kernels into the cooled mashed potato and season with plenty of salt and pepper to taste. Using lightly floured hands, shape the mixture into 12 even-size round cakes, each about 5cm/2in in diameter.

4 When the chicken breast portions are cooked, use a slotted spoon to remove them from the frying pan and keep hot. Melt the butter in the pan and cook the corn cakes for 3 minutes on each side, or until golden and heated through.

5 Meanwhile, mix together the sour cream with the chives in a bowl to make a dip. Transfer the corn cakes from the frying pan to serving plates and top with the chicken breast portions. Serve at once, offering the sour cream with chives on the side.

GLAZED POUSSINS

Golden poussins make an impressive main course and they are also very easy to prepare. A simple mushroom risotto and refreshing side salad are suitable accompaniments.

SERVES FOUR

INGREDIENTS
50g/2oz/¼ cup butter
10ml/2 tsp mixed (apple pie) spice
30ml/2 tbsp clear honey
grated rind and juice of
  2 clementines
4 poussins, each weighing about
  450g/1lb
1 onion, finely chopped
1 garlic clove, chopped
15ml/1 tbsp plain (all-purpose) flour
50ml/2fl oz/¼ cup Marsala
300ml/½ pint/1¼ cups chicken stock
small bunch of fresh coriander
  (cilantro), to garnish

VARIATION
To give the poussins extra flavour, stuff each poussin before roasting with a quartered clementine and one or two garlic cloves, then skewer the legs with sprigs of fresh rosemary.

1 Preheat the oven to 220°C/425°F/Gas 7. Heat the butter, mixed spice, honey and clementine rind and juice until the butter has melted, stirring to mix well. Remove from the heat.

2 Place the poussins in a roasting pan, brush them with the glaze, then roast for 40 minutes. Brush with any remaining glaze and baste occasionally with the pan juices during cooking. Transfer the poussins to a serving platter, cover with foil and stand for 10 minutes.

3 Skim off all but 15ml/1 tbsp of the fat from the roasting pan. Add the onion and garlic to the juices in the pan and cook on the hob (stovetop) until just beginning to brown. Stir in the flour, then gradually pour in the Marsala, followed by the stock, whisking all the time. Bring to the boil and simmer for 3 minutes to make a smooth, rich gravy.

4 Transfer the poussins to warm plates or a platter and garnish with coriander. Offer the gravy separately.

SPATCHCOCK POUSSINS <u>WITH</u> HERBES <u>DE</u> PROVENCE BUTTER

Spatchcock is said to be a distortion of an 18th-century Irish expression "dispatch cock" for providing an unexpected guest with a quick and simple meal. A young chicken was prepared without frills or fuss by being split, flattened and fried or grilled.

SERVES TWO

INGREDIENTS
2 poussins, each weighing about
  450g/1lb
1 shallot, finely chopped
2 garlic cloves, crushed
45ml/3 tbsp chopped mixed fresh
  herbs, such as flat leaf parsley,
  sage, rosemary and thyme
75g/3oz/6 tbsp butter, softened
salt and ground black pepper

VARIATIONS
Add some finely chopped chilli or a little grated lemon rind to the butter.

1 To spatchcock a poussin, place it breast down on a chopping board and split it along the back. Open out the bird and turn it over, so that the breast side is uppermost. Press the bird as flat as possible, then thread two metal skewers through it, across the breast and thigh, to keep it flat. Repeat with the second poussin and place the skewered birds on a grill (broiler) pan.

2 Add the chopped shallot, crushed garlic and chopped mixed herbs to the butter with plenty of seasoning, and then beat well. Dot the butter over the spatchcock poussins.

3 Preheat the grill to high and cook the poussins for 30 minutes, turning them over halfway through. Turn again and baste with the cooking juices, then cook for a further 5–7 minutes on each side.

THAI CHICKEN CURRY

THIS FLAVOURFUL AND FRAGRANT, CREAMY CURRY IS QUITE SIMPLE TO MAKE EVEN THOUGH IT INCLUDES A VARIETY OF INTERESTING INGREDIENTS.

SERVES SIX

INGREDIENTS
    400ml/14oz can unsweetened
      coconut milk
    6 skinless, boneless chicken breast
      portions, finely sliced
    225g/8oz can bamboo shoots,
      drained and sliced
    30ml/2 tbsp fish sauce
    15ml/1 tbsp soft light
      brown sugar
For the green curry paste
    4 green chillies, seeded
    1 lemon grass stalk, sliced
    1 small onion, sliced
    3 garlic cloves
    1cm/½in piece galangal or fresh root
      ginger, peeled
    grated rind of ½ lime
    5ml/1 tsp coriander seeds
    5ml/1 tsp cumin seeds
    2.5ml/½ tsp shrimp or fish sauce
To garnish
    1 red chilli, seeded and cut into
      fine strips
    finely pared rind of ½ lime,
      finely shredded
    fresh Thai purple basil or coriander
      (cilantro), coarsely chopped
To serve
    175g/6oz/scant 1 cup Thai jasmine rice
    pinch of saffron strands

1 First make the green curry paste: put the chillies, lemon grass, onion, garlic, galangal or ginger, lime rind, coriander seeds, cumin seeds and shrimp or fish sauce in a food processor or blender and process until they are reduced to a thick paste. Set aside.

2 Bring half the coconut milk to the boil in a large frying pan, then reduce the heat and simmer for about 5 minutes, or until reduced by half. Stir in the green curry paste and simmer for a further 5 minutes.

3 Add the finely sliced chicken breast portions to the pan with the remaining coconut milk, bamboo shoots, fish sauce and sugar. Stir well to combine all the ingredients and bring the curry back to simmering point, then simmer gently for about 10 minutes, or until the chicken slices are cooked through. The mixture will look grainy or curdled during cooking, but do not worry as this is quite normal.

4 Meanwhile, prepare the garnish and set aside. Add the rice and saffron to a pan of boiling salted water. Reduce the heat and simmer for 10 minutes, or until tender. Drain the rice and serve it with the curry, garnished with the chilli, lime rind and basil or coriander.

GUINEA FOWL WITH WHISKY CREAM SAUCE

SERVED WITH CREAMY SWEET POTATO MASH AND WHOLE BABY LEEKS, GUINEA FOWL IS SUPERB WITH A RICH, CREAMY WHISKY SAUCE.

SERVES FOUR

INGREDIENTS
   2 guinea fowl, each weighing about
     1kg/2¼lb
   90ml/6 tbsp whisky
   150ml/¼ pint/⅔ cup chicken stock
   150ml/¼ pint/⅔ cup double
     (heavy) cream
   20 baby leeks
   salt and ground black pepper
   fresh thyme sprigs, to garnish
   mashed sweet potatoes, to serve

1 Preheat the oven to 200°C/400°F/ Gas 6. Place the guinea fowl in a large roasting pan and brown on all sides on the hob (stovetop), then turn them breast uppermost and transfer the pan to the oven. Roast for 1 hour, until the guinea fowl are golden and cooked through. Transfer the fowl to a serving dish, cover with foil and keep warm.

4 Carve the guinea fowl. To serve, place portions of mashed sweet potato on warmed serving plates, then add the carved meat and the leeks. Garnish with sprigs of fresh thyme, and season with plenty of freshly ground black pepper. Spoon a little of the sauce over each portion and serve the rest separately.

2 Pour off the excess fat from the pan, then heat the juices on the hob and stir in the whisky. Bring to the boil and cook until reduced. Add the stock and cream and simmer again until reduced slightly. Strain and season to taste.

3 Meanwhile, trim the leeks so that they are roughly the same length as the guinea fowl breast portions, then cook them whole in boiling salted water for 3 minutes, or until tender but not too soft. Drain the leeks in a colander.

VARIATION
If you don't like the flavour of whisky, then substitute brandy, Madeira or Marsala. Or, to make a non-alcoholic version, use freshly squeezed orange juice instead.

TURKEY AND CRANBERRY BUNDLES

AFTER THE TRADITIONAL CHRISTMAS OR THANKSGIVING MEAL, IT IS EASY TO END UP WITH LOTS OF TURKEY LEFTOVERS. THESE DELICIOUS FILO PASTRY PARCELS ARE A MARVELLOUS WAY OF USING UP THE SMALL PIECES OF COOKED TURKEY.

2 Cut the filo sheets in half widthways and trim to make 18 squares. Layer three pieces of pastry together, brushing them with a little melted butter so that they stick together. Repeat with the remaining filo squares to give six pieces.

3 Divide the turkey mixture among the pastry, making small piles in the centre of each piece. Gather up the pastry to enclose the filling in neat bundles. Place on a baking sheet, brush with melted butter and bake for 20 minutes, or until the pastry is crisp and golden. Serve hot or warm with a green salad.

VARIATIONS

These little parcels can be made with a variety of fillings and are great for using up left-over cooked meats. To make Ham and Cheddar Bundles, replace the turkey with ham and use Cheddar in place of the Brie. A fruit-flavoured chutney would make a good alternative to the cranberry sauce. Alternatively, to make Chicken and Stilton Bundles, use cooked chicken in place of the turkey and white Stilton instead of Brie. Replace the cranberry sauce with mango chutney.

SERVES SIX

INGREDIENTS
   450g/1lb cooked turkey, cut
     into chunks
   115g/4oz/1 cup Brie, diced
   30ml/2 tbsp cranberry sauce
   30ml/2 tbsp chopped fresh parsley
   9 sheets filo pastry, 45 × 28cm/
     18 × 11in each, thawed if frozen
   50g/2oz/¼ cup butter, melted
   salt and ground black pepper
   green salad, to serve

1 Preheat the oven to 200ºC/400ºF/ Gas 6. Mix the turkey, Brie, cranberry sauce and chopped parsley. Season with salt and pepper.

[MONDAY]

Chicken and Leek Pie

SERVES	PREP	COOK
4 PEOPLE	**15** MINS	**55** MINS

One serving provides...

518	10g	19g	4g	1.8g
Calories	Sugar	Fat	Saturates	Salt
26%	11%	27%	20%	30%

of your guideline daily amount

For the filling
• 1 tbsp olive oil
• 3 medium leeks, trimmed and sliced
• 150g mushrooms, sliced
• 1 red pepper, deseeded and thinly sliced
• 400g cooked chicken, torn into bite-sized pieces
• 1 tsp dried tarragon
• 450ml chicken stock or one stock cube
• 300g can condensed mushroom soup

For the topping
• 600g potatoes, peeled and grated
• 300g sweet potatoes, peeled and grated
• 25g sunflower spread
• 1 tbsp olive oil
• salt and freshly ground black pepper
• 4 spring onions, trimmed and thinly sliced

1 Preheat the oven to 190°C/375°F/Gas 5.
2 Heat the olive oil in a pan and add the leeks, mushrooms and red pepper. Stir-fry over a medium heat until beginning to soften. Add the chicken and tarragon then pour the stock over and bring to the boil. Simmer for 10 minutes, add the condensed soup and stir well. Heat until bubbling then spoon into a heatproof casserole dish.
3 While the pie filling is cooking, bring a large pan of water to the boil. Plunge the potatoes and sweet potatoes into the boiling water for 1 minute then drain through a sieve and tip into a mixing bowl. Add the sunflower spread, olive oil, seasoning and spring onions and mix well.
4 Spread over the chicken pie filling and bake for 35 minutes until the topping is beginning to turn golden. Serve immediately.

You can serve this with any leftover broccoli from Sunday's roast.

Roast chickens are available at the oven-fresh counter in store

[SUNDAY]

Garlic Roast Chicken

SERVES 4 PEOPLE	PREP 30 MINS	COOK 2 HRS

One serving provides...

600 Calories	19g Sugar	19g Fat	3g Saturates	0.6g Salt
30%	21%	27%	15%	10%

of your guideline daily amount

- 2kg (approx.) chicken
- 6 cloves garlic, peeled and thinly sliced
- salt and freshly ground black pepper
- 1 tbsp sunflower oil

For the vegetables
- 2kg butternut squash, peeled, deseeded and cut into chunks
- 3 tbsp olive oil
- salt and freshly ground black pepper
- 700g broccoli
- 25g sunflower seeds
- finely grated zest of 1 orange

1 Preheat the oven to 200°C/400°F/Gas 6.
2 Place a trivet into a roasting pan and lift the chicken onto it. Using clean hands, push slivers of the sliced garlic between the skin and flesh of the bird, all around the breast. Season well and rub all over with the sunflower oil. Place the chicken in the preheated oven and roast as per the on-pack cooking instructions.
3 Toss the squash with the olive oil and a little seasoning and roast with the chicken for the final 35 minutes of cooking time.
4 About 15 minutes before the chicken is cooked, divide the broccoli into small florets and place into a steamer. Steam for 12 minutes. Meanwhile, place the sunflower seeds on a baking tray in the hot oven with a little oil, until lightly browned. Mix with the broccoli and orange zest just before serving. Serve slices of roast chicken with roasted butternut squash and broccoli.

As it's a large chicken, there should be enough leftover for Monday's Chicken and Leek Pie (overleaf).

TURKEY LASAGNE

THIS EASY MEAL-IN-ONE PASTA BAKE IS DELICIOUS MADE WITH COOKED TURKEY PIECES AND BROCCOLI IN A RICH, CREAMY PARMESAN SAUCE.

SERVES FOUR

INGREDIENTS

    30ml/2 tbsp light olive oil
    1 onion, chopped
    2 garlic cloves, chopped
    450g/1lb cooked turkey meat,
      finely diced
    225g/8oz/1 cup mascarpone cheese
    30ml/2 tbsp chopped fresh tarragon
    300g/11oz broccoli, broken
      into florets
    salt and ground black pepper
For the sauce
    50g/2oz/¼ cup butter
    30ml/2 tbsp plain (all-purpose) flour
    600ml/1 pint/2½ cups milk
    75g/3oz/1 cup freshly grated
      Parmesan cheese
    115g/4oz no pre-cook lasagne verdi

3 To make the sauce, melt the butter in a pan, stir in the flour and cook for about 1 minute, still stirring. Remove from the heat and gradually stir in the milk. Return to the heat and bring the sauce to the boil, stirring continuously. Simmer for 1 minute, then add 50g/2oz/⅔ cup of the Parmesan and plenty of salt and pepper.

4 Spoon a layer of the turkey mixture into a large, shallow baking dish. Add a layer of broccoli and cover with sheets of lasagne. Coat with cheese sauce. Repeat these layers, finishing with a layer of cheese sauce on top. Sprinkle with the remaining Parmesan and bake for 35–40 minutes.

1 Preheat the oven to 180°C/350°F/ Gas 4. Heat the oil in a heavy pan and cook the onion and garlic until softened but not coloured. Remove the pan from the heat and stir in the turkey, mascarpone cheese and tarragon, with seasoning to taste.

2 Blanch the broccoli in a large pan of salted boiling water for 1 minute, then drain and rinse thoroughly under cold water to prevent the broccoli from overcooking. Drain well and set aside.

COOK'S TIP
This is a delicious way of using up any cooked turkey that is left over after Christmas or Thanksgiving celebrations. It is also especially good made with half ham and half turkey.

STIR-FRIED DUCK WITH PINEAPPLE

THE FATTY SKIN ON DUCK MAKES IT IDEAL FOR STIR-FRYING: AS SOON AS THE DUCK IS ADDED TO THE HOT PAN THE FAT IS RELEASED, CREATING DELICIOUS CRISP SKIN AND TENDER FLESH WHEN COOKED. STIR-FRIED VEGETABLES AND NOODLES MAKE THIS A MEAL IN ITSELF.

SERVES FOUR

INGREDIENTS

    250g/9oz fresh sesame noodles
    2 duck breast portions, sliced
    3 spring onions (scallions), cut
      into strips
    2 celery sticks, cut into strips
    1 fresh pineapple, peeled, cored and
      cut into strips
    300g/11oz mixed vegetables, such as
      carrots, (bell) peppers, beansprouts
      and cabbage, cut into strips
    90ml/6 tbsp plum sauce

1 Cook the noodles in a pan of boiling water for 3 minutes. Drain.

2 Meanwhile, heat a wok. Add the duck to the hot wok and stir-fry for about 2 minutes, until crisp. If the duck yields a lot of fat, drain off all but 30ml/2 tbsp.

3 Add the spring onions and celery to the wok and stir-fry for 2 minutes more. Use a slotted spoon to remove the ingredients from the wok and set aside. Add the pineapple strips and mixed vegetables, and stir-fry for 2 minutes.

4 Add the cooked noodles and plum sauce to the wok, then replace the duck, spring onion and celery mixture.

5 Stir-fry the duck mixture for about 2 minutes more, or until the noodles and vegetables are hot and the duck is cooked through. Serve at once.

COOK'S TIP

Fresh sesame noodles can be bought from large supermarkets – you'll find them in the chiller cabinets alongside fresh pasta. If they aren't available, then use fresh egg noodles instead and cook according to the instructions on the packet. For extra flavour, add a little sesame oil to the cooking water.

WARM DUCK SALAD <u>WITH</u> POACHED EGGS

THIS SALAD LOOKS SPECTACULAR AND TASTES DIVINE, AND MAKES A PERFECT CELEBRATION FIRST COURSE OR, ACCOMPANIED BY WARM CRUSTY BREAD, A LIGHT LUNCH OR SUPPER DISH.

SERVES FOUR

INGREDIENTS

   3 skinless, boneless duck breast
     portions, thinly sliced
   30ml/2 tbsp soy sauce
   30ml/2 tbsp balsamic vinegar
   30ml/2 tbsp groundnut oil
   25g/1oz/2 tbsp unsalted
     (sweet) butter
   1 shallot, finely chopped
   115g/4oz/1½ cups chanterelle
     mushrooms
   4 eggs
   50g/2oz mixed salad leaves
   salt and ground black pepper
   30ml/2 tbsp extra virgin olive oil,
     to serve

1 Toss the duck in the soy sauce and balsamic vinegar. Cover and chill for 30 minutes to allow the duck to absorb the flavours. Soak 12 bamboo skewers (13cm/5in long) in water to help prevent them from burning during cooking.

2 Preheat the grill (broiler). Thread the duck slices on to the skewers, pleating them neatly. Place on a grill pan and drizzle with half the oil. Grill (broil) for 3–5 minutes, then turn the skewers and drizzle with the remaining oil. Grill for a further 3 minutes, or until the duck is cooked through and golden.

VARIATION
Instead of threading the duck strips on to skewers, simply stir-fry in a little oil for a few minutes until crisp and cooked through, then scatter over the salad leaves with the mushrooms.

3 Meanwhile, melt the butter in a frying pan and cook the finely chopped shallot until softened but not coloured. Add the chanterelle mushrooms and cook over a high heat for about 5 minutes, stirring occasionally.

4 Poach the eggs while the chanterelles are cooking. Half fill a frying pan with water, add salt and heat until simmering. Break the eggs one at a time into a cup before tipping carefully into the water. Poach the eggs gently for about 3 minutes, or until the whites are set. Use a slotted spoon to transfer the eggs to a warm plate and trim off any untidy white.

5 Arrange the salad leaves on serving plates, then add the chanterelles and skewered duck. Carefully add the poached eggs. Drizzle with olive oil and season with ground black pepper, then serve at once.

MARMALADE-GLAZED GOOSE

SUCCULENT ROAST GOOSE IS THE CLASSIC CENTREPIECE FOR A TRADITIONAL CHRISTMAS LUNCH.
RED CABBAGE COOKED WITH LEEKS, AND BRAISED FENNEL ARE TASTY ACCOMPANIMENTS.

SERVES EIGHT

INGREDIENTS
4.5kg/10lb oven-ready goose
1 cooking apple, peeled, cored and
   cut into eighths
1 large onion, cut into eighths
bunch of fresh sage, plus extra sprigs
   to garnish
30ml/2 tbsp ginger
   marmalade, melted
salt and ground black pepper
For the stuffing
   25g/1oz/2 tbsp butter
   1 onion, finely chopped
   15ml/1 tbsp ginger marmalade
   450g/1lb/2 cups ready-to-eat
      prunes, chopped
   45ml/3 tbsp Madeira
   225g/8oz/4 cups fresh white
      breadcrumbs
   30ml/2 tbsp chopped fresh sage
For the gravy
   1 onion, chopped
   15ml/1 tbsp plain (all-purpose) flour
   150ml/¼ pint/⅔ cup Madeira
   600ml/1 pint/2½ cups chicken stock

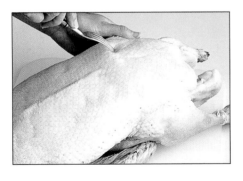

1 Preheat the oven to 200°C/400°F/
Gas 6. Prick the skin of the goose all
over with a fork and season the bird
generously, both inside and out.

COOK'S TIP
Red cabbage goes well with goose. Cook
1 small leek, sliced, in 75g/3oz/6 tbsp
butter, add 1kg/2¼lb/9 cups shredded
red cabbage, with the grated rind of
1 orange, and cook for 2 minutes. Add
30ml/2 tbsp Madeira and 15ml/1 tbsp
brown sugar and cook for 15 minutes.

2 Mix the apple, onion and sage leaves
and spoon the mixture into the parson's
(pope's) nose end of the goose.

3 To make the stuffing, melt the butter
in a large pan and cook the onion for
about 5 minutes, or until softened but
not coloured. Remove the pan from
the heat and stir in the marmalade,
chopped prunes, Madeira, breadcrumbs
and chopped sage.

4 Stuff the neck end of the goose with
some of the prepared stuffing, and set
the remaining stuffing aside in the
refrigerator. Sew up the bird or secure
it with skewers to prevent the stuffing
from escaping during cooking.

5 Place the goose in a large roasting
pan. Butter a piece of foil and use to
cover the goose loosely, then place in
the oven for 2 hours.

6 Baste the goose frequently during
cooking and remove excess fat from the
pan as necessary, using a small ladle or
serving spoon. (Strain, cool and chill the
fat in a covered container: it is excellent
for roasting potatoes.)

7 Remove the foil from the goose and
brush the melted ginger marmalade
over the goose, then roast for 30–40
minutes more, or until cooked through.
To check if the goose is cooked, pierce
the thick part of the thigh with a metal
skewer; the juices will run clear when the
bird is cooked. Remove from the oven
and cover with foil, then leave to stand
for 15 minutes before carving.

8 While the goose is cooking, shape the
remaining stuffing into walnut-size balls
and place them in an ovenproof dish.
Spoon 30ml/2 tbsp of the goose fat over
the stuffing balls and bake for about
15 minutes before the goose is cooked.

9 To make the gravy, pour off all but
15ml/1 tbsp of fat from the roasting
pan, leaving the meat juices behind.
Add the onion and cook for 3–5 minutes,
or until softened but not coloured.
Sprinkle in the flour and then gradually
stir in the Madeira and stock. Bring to
the boil, stirring continuously, then
simmer for 3 minutes, or until thickened
and glossy. Strain the gravy and serve it
with the carved goose and stuffing.
Garnish with sage leaves.

GAME AND NEW MEAT DISHES

Game birds and animals have rich, distinctive flavours and are often cooked to make robust and warming dishes. Traditional dishes abound in this chapter, with classics such as Roast Pheasant, Rich Game Pie and Wild Duck with Olives, as well as exciting new ideas, such as Grilled Spiced Quail with Mixed Leaf and Mushroom Salad. Exotic meats such as crocodile, kangaroo and wild boar are richly flavoured, yet lean and healthy, and lend themselves to all sorts of cooking methods. Try Roast Stuffed Fillets of Crocodile, crisp deep-fried Goujons of Ostrich with Fries and Lemon Mayonnaise, or griddled Marinated Alligator Steaks with Cajun Vegetables.

ROAST PHEASANT

The hen pheasant has plump, juicy and tender flesh, making it suitable for roasting. All pheasant contain very little fat, however, so it is important to ensure that the meat stays moist during cooking. A layer of fatty bacon covering the breast helps it stay succulent.

SERVES TWO

INGREDIENTS
  1 hen pheasant
  25g/1oz/2 tbsp butter
  115g/4oz rindless streaky (fatty)
    bacon rashers (strips)
  salt and ground black pepper
  chips (French fries), to serve
For the stuffing
  25g/1oz/2 tbsp butter
  1 leek, chopped
  115g/4oz peeled, cooked chestnuts,
    coarsely chopped (see Cook's Tip)
  30ml/2 tbsp chopped fresh flat
    leaf parsley
For the gravy
  15ml/1 tbsp cornflour (cornstarch)
  300ml/½ pint/1¼ cups well-flavoured
    chicken stock
  50ml/2fl oz/¼ cup port

1 Preheat the oven to 190°C/375°F/ Gas 5. Season the pheasant inside and out with plenty of salt and pepper.

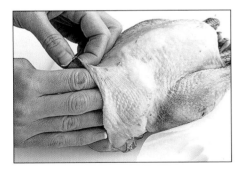

2 Carefully loosen and lift the skin covering the breast and rub the butter between the skin and flesh.

COOK'S TIP
For convenience, it is much easier to use vacuum-packed chestnuts rather than fresh, which are fiddly to peel and cook. Simply rinse the chestnuts thoroughly with boiling water and drain before using. Whole, unsweetened canned chestnuts could be used, but these are fairly dense and much softer than the vacuum-packed version.

3 To make the stuffing, melt the butter in a pan and, when foaming, add the leek. Cook for about 5 minutes, or until softened but not coloured. Remove the pan from the heat, and mix in the cooked, chopped chestnuts, parsley and seasoning to taste.

4 Spoon the stuffing into the body cavity of the pheasant and secure the opening with skewers. Arrange the bacon rashers in a lattice pattern over the breast. Place in a roasting pan.

5 Roast the pheasant for 1–1½ hours, or until the juices run clear when the bird is pierced with a skewer in the thickest part of the leg.

6 Remove the pheasant from the oven and cover closely with foil, then leave to stand in a warm place for 15 minutes before carving.

7 Meanwhile, heat the juices in the roasting pan on the hob (stovetop) and stir in the cornflour to form a paste. Gradually pour in the stock and port, stirring continuously. Bring to the boil, then reduce the heat and simmer for about 5 minutes, or until the sauce is slightly thickened and glossy.

8 Strain the sauce into a sauce boat or serving jug and keep warm while you carve the pheasant, then serve the pheasant with the stuffing and gravy. Crisp, deep-fried matchstick potato chips (French fries) or game chips would make a good accompaniment.

GRILLED SPICED QUAIL WITH MIXED LEAF AND MUSHROOM SALAD

THIS IS A PERFECT SUPPER DISH FOR AUTUMNAL ENTERTAINING. QUAIL IS AT ITS BEST WHEN THE BREAST MEAT IS REMOVED FROM THE CARCASS, SO THAT IT COOKS QUICKLY AND CAN BE SERVED RARE.

SERVES FOUR

INGREDIENTS

   8 quail breast portions
   50g/2oz/¼ cup butter
   5ml/1 tsp paprika
   salt and ground black pepper
For the salad
   60ml/4 tbsp walnut oil
   30ml/2 tbsp olive oil
   45ml/3 tbsp balsamic vinegar
   25g/1oz/2 tbsp butter
   75g/3oz/generous 1 cup chanterelle
     mushrooms, sliced, if large
   25g/1oz/3 tbsp walnut
     halves, toasted
   115g/4oz mixed salad leaves

1 Preheat the grill (broiler). Arrange the quail on the grill rack, skin-sides up. Dot with half the butter and sprinkle with half the paprika and a little salt.

2 Grill the quail breast portions for 3 minutes, then turn them over and dot with the remaining butter, then sprinkle with the remaining paprika and a little salt. Grill for a further 3 minutes, or until cooked. Transfer the quail breasts to a warmed dish, cover and leave to stand while preparing the salad.

COOK'S TIP
Take care when roasting the walnuts as they scorch quickly and will become bitter if over-browned. The best way to roast them is to heat a non-stick frying pan until hot. Add the walnuts and cook for 3–5 minutes, or until golden, turning them frequently.

3 Make the dressing first. Whisk the oils with the balsamic vinegar, then season and set aside. Heat the butter until foaming and cook the chanterelles for about 3 minutes, or until just beginning to soften. Add the walnuts and heat through. Remove from the heat.

4 Thinly slice the cooked quail breast portions and arrange them on four individual serving plates with the warmed chanterelle mushrooms and walnuts and mixed salad leaves. Drizzle the oil and vinegar dressing over the salad and serve warm.

MARINATED PIGEON IN RED WINE

THE TIME TAKEN TO MARINATE AND COOK THIS CASSEROLE IS WELL REWARDED BY THE FABULOUS RICH FLAVOUR OF THE FINISHED DISH. STIR-FRIED GREEN CABBAGE AND CELERIAC PURÉE ARE DELICIOUS WITH PIGEON CASSEROLE.

SERVES FOUR

INGREDIENTS

    4 pigeons, each weighing about
      225g/8oz
    30ml/2 tbsp olive oil
    1 onion, coarsely chopped
    225g/8oz/3¼ cups chestnut
      mushrooms, sliced
    15ml/1 tbsp plain (all-purpose) flour
    300ml/½ pint/1¼ cups game stock
    30ml/2 tbsp chopped fresh parsley
    salt and ground black pepper
    flat leaf parsley, to garnish
For the marinade
    15ml/1 tbsp light olive oil
    1 onion, chopped
    1 carrot, peeled and chopped
    1 celery stick, chopped
    3 garlic cloves, sliced
    6 allspice berries, bruised
    2 bay leaves
    8 black peppercorns, bruised
    150ml/¼ pint/⅔ cup red wine vinegar
    150ml/¼ pint/⅔ cup red wine
    45ml/3 tbsp redcurrant jelly

1 Mix all the ingredients for the marinade in a large dish. Add the pigeons and turn them in the marinade, then cover and chill for 12 hours, turning the pigeons frequently.

VARIATION
If you are unable to buy pigeon, this recipe works equally well with rabbit or hare. Buy portions and make deep slashes in the flesh so that the marinade soaks into, and flavours right to, the centre of the pieces of meat.

2 Preheat the oven to 150°C/300°F/ Gas 2. Heat the oil in a large, flameproof casserole and gently cook the onion and mushrooms for about 5 minutes, or until the onion has softened.

3 Meanwhile, drain the pigeons and strain the marinade into a bowl, then set both aside separately.

4 Sprinkle the flour over the pigeons and add them to the casserole, breast-sides down. Pour in the marinade and stock, and add the chopped parsley and seasoning. Cover and cook for 2½ hours.

5 Check the seasoning, then serve the pigeons on warmed plates and ladle the sauce over them. Garnish with parsley.

PAN-FRIED PHEASANT WITH OATMEAL AND CREAMY MUSTARD SAUCE

OATMEAL IS OFTEN USED FOR COATING FISH BEFORE PAN FRYING, BUT IT IS EQUALLY GOOD WITH TENDER POULTRY, GAME AND OTHER MEATS. INSTEAD OF A HEAVY EGG BASE, SWEET, SLIGHTLY TANGY REDCURRANT JELLY IS USED TO BIND THE OATMEAL TO THE TENDER PHEASANT BREAST FILLETS.

SERVES FOUR

INGREDIENTS
115g/4oz/1 cup medium oatmeal
4 skinless boneless pheasant breasts
45ml/3 tbsp redcurrant jelly, melted
50g/2oz/¼ cup butter
15ml/1 tbsp olive oil
45ml/3 tbsp wholegrain mustard
300ml/½ pint/1¼ cups double
  (heavy) cream
salt and ground black pepper

1 Place the oatmeal on a plate and season well. Brush the pheasant breasts with redcurrant jelly, then turn them in the oatmeal to coat them evenly.

2 Heat the butter and oil in a frying pan until foaming. Add the oatmeal-coated pheasant breast portions and cook over a high heat until golden brown on both sides. Reduce the heat and cook for a further 8–10 minutes.

3 Stir the mustard and cream into the pan, stirring it into the cooking juices. Bring slowly to the boil, then simmer for 10 minutes, or until the sauce has thickened and the pheasant breast portions are cooked through.

WILD DUCK WITH OLIVES

COMPARED TO FARMED DUCK, WILD DUCK, WHICH HAS A BRILLIANT FLAVOUR, IS WORTH THE EXTRA EXPENSE FOR A SPECIAL OCCASION MEAL. THESE ARE QUITE SMALL BIRDS, SO ALLOW TWO PIECES PER PORTION. MASHED PARSNIPS AND GREEN VEGETABLES ARE GOOD WITH THE DUCK.

SERVES TWO

INGREDIENTS
1 wild duck, weighing about
  1.5kg/3¼lb, cut into 4 portions
1 onion, chopped
1 carrot, chopped
2 celery sticks, chopped
4 garlic cloves, sliced
1 bottle red wine
300ml/½ pint/1¼ cups game stock
small handful of fresh thyme leaves
2.5ml/½ tsp arrowroot
225g/8oz/2 cups pitted green olives
115g/4oz passata (bottled
  strained tomatoes)
salt and ground black pepper

1 Preheat the oven to 220°C/425°F/ Gas 7. Season the duck portions with salt and pepper and place them in a large flameproof casserole.

2 Roast the duck for 20 minutes, then remove the casserole from the oven. Use a slotted spoon to remove the duck from the casserole and set aside. Reduce the oven temperature to 160°C/ 325°F/Gas 3.

3 Carefully transfer the casserole to the hob (stovetop) and heat the fat until it is sizzling. Add the onion, carrot, celery and garlic, and cook for 10 minutes, or until the vegetables are softened. Pour in the wine and boil until it has reduced by about half.

4 Add the stock and thyme leaves, then replace the duck portions in the casserole. Bring to the boil, skim the surface, then cover the casserole and place in the oven for about 1 hour, or until the duck is tender. Remove the duck portions and keep warm.

5 Skim the excess fat from the cooking liquid, strain it and return it to the casserole, then bring it to the boil. Skim the liquid again, if necessary.

6 Mix the arrowroot to a thin paste with a little cold water and whisk it into the simmering sauce. Add the olives and passata and replace the duck, then cook, uncovered, for 15 minutes. Check the seasoning and serve.

GROUSE WITH ORCHARD FRUIT STUFFING

TART APPLES, PLUMS AND PEARS MAKE A FABULOUS ORCHARD FRUIT STUFFING THAT COMPLEMENTS THE RICH GAMEY FLAVOUR OF GROUSE PERFECTLY.

2 Add the shallots to the fat remaining in the casserole and cook until softened but not coloured. Add the apple, pear, plums and mixed spice, and cook for about 5 minutes, or until the fruits are just beginning to soften. Remove the casserole from the heat and spoon the hot fruit mixture into the body cavities of the birds.

3 Truss the birds neatly with string. Smear the remaining butter over the birds and wrap them in the chard leaves, then replace them in the casserole.

4 Pour in the Marsala and heat until simmering. Cover tightly and simmer for 20 minutes, or until the birds are tender, taking care not to overcook them. Leave to rest in a warm place for about 10 minutes before serving.

COOK'S TIP
There isn't a lot of liquid in the casserole for cooking the birds – they are steamed rather than boiled, so it is very important that the casserole is heavy-based with a tight-fitting lid, otherwise the liquid may evaporate and the chard burn on the base of the pan.

SERVES TWO

INGREDIENTS
  juice of ½ lemon
  2 young grouse
  50g/2oz/¼ cup butter
  4 Swiss chard leaves
  50ml/2fl oz/¼ cup Marsala
  salt and ground black pepper
For the stuffing
  2 shallots, finely chopped
  1 cooking apple, peeled, cored
    and chopped
  1 pear, peeled, cored
    and chopped
  2 plums, halved, stoned (pitted)
    and chopped
  large pinch of mixed (apple pie)
    spice

1 Sprinkle the lemon juice over the grouse and season it with salt and black pepper. Melt half the butter in a large flameproof casserole, add the grouse and cook for about 10 minutes, or until browned, turning occasionally. Use tongs to remove the grouse from the casserole and set aside.

HARE POT PIES

THE FULL, GAMEY FLAVOUR OF HARE IS PERFECT FOR THIS DISH; HOWEVER, BONELESS VENISON, RABBIT, PHEASANT OR ANY OTHER GAME MEAT CAN BE USED IN THIS RECIPE. A LARGE PIE CAN BE MADE INSTEAD OF INDIVIDUAL POT PIES, IF YOU PREFER.

SERVES FOUR

INGREDIENTS
   30ml/2 tbsp olive oil
   1 leek, sliced
   225g/8oz parsnips, sliced
   225g/8oz carrots, sliced
   1 fennel bulb, sliced
   675g/1½lb boneless hare, diced
   30ml/2 tbsp plain (all-purpose) flour
   60ml/4 tbsp Madeira
   300ml/½ pint/1¼ cups game or
      chicken stock
   45ml/3 tbsp chopped fresh parsley
   salt and ground black pepper
For the topping
   450g/1lb puff pastry, thawed if frozen
   1 egg yolk, beaten, to glaze

1 Heat the olive oil in a large, flameproof casserole, add the sliced leek, parsnips, carrots and fennel and cook for about 10 minutes, stirring frequently, or until the vegetables are softened. Use a slotted spoon to remove the vegetables from the casserole and set aside.

2 Add the hare to the casserole in batches and stir-fry over a high heat for 10 minutes, or until browned. When all the meat is browned, return it to the pan. Sprinkle in the flour and stir in the Madeira and stock. Return the cooked vegetables to the casserole with the seasoning and parsley. Heat until simmering, then cook for 20 minutes.

3 Preheat the oven to 220°C/425°F/ Gas 7. Spoon the hare mixture into four individual pie dishes. Cut the pastry into quarters and roll out on a lightly floured work surface to cover the pies, making the pieces larger than the dishes. Trim off the excess pastry and use the trimmings to line the rim of each dish. Dampen the pastry rims with cold water and cover with the pastry lids. Pinch the edges together to seal in the filling. Brush with beaten egg yolk and make a small hole in the top of each pie to allow steam to escape.

4 Bake for 25 minutes, or until the pastry is risen and golden. If necessary, cover the pastry with foil after 15 minutes to prevent it from overbrowning.

RICH GAME PIE

TERRIFIC FOR STYLISH PICNICS OR JUST AS SMART FOR A FORMAL WEDDING BUFFET, THIS PIE LOOKS SPECTACULAR WHEN BAKED IN A FLUTED RAISED PIE MOULD. SOME SPECIALIST KITCHEN SHOPS HIRE THE MOULDS TO AVOID THE EXPENSE OF PURCHASING THEM; ALTERNATIVELY A 20CM/8IN ROUND SPRINGFORM TIN CAN BE USED.

SERVES TEN

INGREDIENTS
25g/1oz/2 tbsp butter
1 onion, finely chopped
2 garlic cloves, finely chopped
900g/2lb mixed boneless game
  meat, such as skinless pheasant
  and/or pigeon breast, venison
  and rabbit, diced
30ml/2 tbsp chopped mixed fresh
  herbs such as parsley, thyme
  and marjoram
salt and ground black pepper
For the pâté
50g/2oz/¼ cup butter
2 garlic cloves, finely chopped
450g/1lb chicken livers, rinsed,
  trimmed and chopped
60ml/4 tbsp brandy
5ml/1 tsp ground mace
For the hot water crust pastry
675g/1½lb/6 cups strong white
  bread flour
5ml/1 tsp salt
115ml/3½fl oz/scant ½ cup milk
115ml/3½fl oz/scant ½ cup water
115g/4oz/½ cup lard
  (shortening), diced
115g/4oz/½ cup butter, diced
beaten egg, to glaze
For the jelly
300ml/½ pint/1¼ cups game or
  beef consommé
2.5ml/½ tsp powdered gelatine

1 Melt the butter in a small pan until foaming, then add the onion and garlic, and cook until softened. Remove from the heat and mix with the diced game meat and the chopped mixed herbs. Season well, cover and chill.

2 To make the pâté, melt the butter in a pan. Add the garlic and chicken livers and cook until the livers are just browned. Remove the pan from the heat and stir in the brandy and mace. Purée the mixture in a blender until smooth, then set aside and leave to cool.

3 To make the pastry, sift the flour and salt into a bowl and make a well in the centre. Place the milk and water in a pan. Add the lard and butter and heat gently until melted, then bring to the boil and remove from the heat as soon as the mixture begins to bubble. Pour the hot liquid into the well in the flour and beat until smooth. Cover and leave until cool enough to handle.

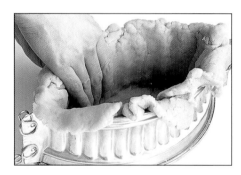

4 Preheat the oven to 200°C/400°F/Gas 6. Roll out two-thirds of the pastry and use to line a 23cm/9in raised pie mould. Spoon in half the game mixture and press it down evenly. Add the pâté and then top with the remaining game.

5 Roll out the remaining pastry to form a lid. Brush the edge of the pastry lining the tin (pan) with a little water and cover the pie with the pastry lid. Trim off excess pastry from around the edge. Pinch the edges together to seal in the filling. Make 2 holes in the centre of the lid and glaze with egg. Use pastry trimmings to roll out leaves to garnish the pie. Brush with egg.

6 Bake the pie for 20 minutes, then cover the top with foil and cook for a further 10 minutes. Reduce the oven temperature to 150°C/300°F/Gas 2. Glaze the pie again with beaten egg and cook for a further 1½ hours, keeping the top covered loosely with foil.

7 Remove the pie from the oven and leave it to stand for about 15 minutes. Increase the oven temperature to 200°C/400°F/Gas 6. Stand the tin on a baking sheet and remove the sides. Quickly glaze the sides of the pie with beaten egg and cover the top with foil, then cook for a final 15 minutes to brown the sides properly. Leave to cool completely, then chill the pie overnight.

8 To make the jelly, heat the game or beef consommé in a small pan until just beginning to bubble, whisk in the gelatine until dissolved and leave to cool until just setting. Using a small funnel, carefully pour the jellied consommé into the holes in the pie. Chill until set. This pie will keep in the refrigerator for up to 3 days.

MEDALLIONS OF VENISON WITH HERBY HORSERADISH DUMPLINGS

VENISON IS LEAN AND FULL-FLAVOURED. THIS RECIPE MAKES A SPECTACULAR DINNER PARTY DISH — IT GIVES THE APPEARANCE OF BEING DIFFICULT TO MAKE BUT IS ACTUALLY VERY EASY.

SERVES FOUR

INGREDIENTS
  600ml/1 pint/2½ cups venison stock
  120ml/4fl oz/½ cup port
  15ml/1 tbsp sunflower oil
  4 × 175g/6oz medallions of venison
  chopped parsley, to garnish
  steamed baby vegetables, such as
    carrots, courgettes (zucchini) and
    turnips, cooked, to serve
For the dumplings
  75g/3oz/⅔ cup self-raising
    (self-rising) flour
  40g/1½oz beef suet
  15ml/1 tbsp chopped fresh herbs
  5ml/1 tsp creamed horseradish
  45–60ml/3–4 tbsp water

1 First make the dumplings: mix the flour, suet and herbs and make a well in the middle. Add the horseradish and water, then mix to make a soft but not sticky dough. Shape the dough into walnut-sized balls and chill in the refrigerator for up to 1 hour.

2 Boil the venison stock in a pan until reduced by half. Add the port and continue boiling until reduced again by half, then pour the reduced stock into a large frying pan. Heat the stock until it is simmering and add the dumplings. Poach them gently for 5–10 minutes, or until risen and cooked through. Use a slotted spoon to remove the dumplings from the pan.

3 Smear the oil over a non-stick griddle, heat until very hot. Add the venison, cook for 2–3 minutes on each side. Place the venison medallions on warm serving plates and pour the sauce over. Serve with the dumplings and the vegetables, garnished with parsley.

GOUJONS OF OSTRICH WITH FRIES AND LEMON MAYONNAISE

FIRM, MEATY OSTRICH MAKES DELICIOUSLY DIFFERENT GOUJONS, ESPECIALLY WHEN SERVED WITH ZESTY LEMON-FLAVOURED MAYONNAISE AND CRUNCHY CHIPS.

SERVES FOUR

INGREDIENTS
 15ml/1 tbsp plain (all-purpose) flour
 450g/1lb ostrich fillet, cut into
  fine strips
 1 egg white, beaten
 50g/2oz/1 cup fresh white
  breadcrumbs
 sunflower oil, for deep frying
 3 large potatoes, cut into
  thin strips
 grated rind of 1 lemon
 150ml/¼ pint/⅔ cup mayonnaise
 salt and ground black pepper
 herb salad, to serve

1 Season the flour with salt and pepper and place on a plate or in a shallow dish. Dip the ostrich strips first in the flour, then in the beaten egg white and finally in breadcrumbs. It is easier to do this in batches.

2 Heat the sunflower oil for deep-frying in a large, heavy pan or deep-frying pan to 190ºC/375ºF, or until a cube of day-old bread browns in not more than 30–60 seconds.

3 Cook the ostrich goujons in batches for about 5 minutes, or until golden and crisp. Remove from the oil and drain on kitchen paper and keep hot. Reheat the oil and cook the strips of potatoes for about 5–6 minutes, or until crisp and golden. Drain well on kitchen paper.

4 Stir the grated lemon rind into the mayonnaise. Serve the ostrich goujons with the fries and lemon mayonnaise, accompanied by the herb salad.

ROAST STUFFED FILLETS OF CROCODILE

THIS IS A MARVELLOUS, MODERN DINNER-PARTY DISH. CROCODILE IS A HEALTHY, LOW-FAT MEAT AND COOKED IN THIS WAY, IS EASY TO SERVE AND DELICIOUS TO EAT.

SERVES FOUR

INGREDIENTS
  2 × 225g/8oz crocodile fillets
  225g/8oz cooked mixed long grain
    and wild rice
  1 leek, finely chopped
  2 courgettes (zucchini), chopped
  grated rind and juice of
    1 lemon
  a little butter
  45ml/3 tbsp balsamic vinegar
  salt and ground black pepper

VARIATION
Use 450g/1lb alligator fillet, halved, in place of the crocodile fillets.

1 Preheat the oven to 200°C/400°F/ Gas 6. Season the crocodile fillets with coarsely ground sea salt and pepper. Mix together the cooked mixed long grain and wild rice, leek, courgettes and lemon rind.

2 Grease an ovenproof dish with a little butter and lay one crocodile fillet in it. Spoon the rice mixture over the top. Put the other crocodile fillet on top. Press the crocodile fillets together and tie them at regular intervals with fine string to keep the stuffing in place.

3 Pour the lemon juice and balsamic vinegar over, and cover the crocodile with a piece of buttered foil. Roast for 15–20 minutes, or until the crocodile is browned, tender and cooked through.

4 Remove the string and cut the stuffed crocodile into portions. Transfer to warmed plates and serve at once.

MARINATED ALLIGATOR STEAKS WITH CAJUN VEGETABLES

THIS LOUISIANA SPECIALITY MAKES A COLOURFUL — AND FLAVOURFUL — SUPPER DISH.

SERVES FOUR

INGREDIENTS
    4 alligator steaks, cut from the fillet,
      each weighing 175g/6oz
    juice of 2 limes
    1 shallot, sliced
    1 fresh red chilli, seeded
      and chopped
    30ml/2 tbsp soy sauce
    30ml/2 tbsp sesame oil
    chopped fresh coriander (cilantro),
      to garnish
For the Cajun vegetables
    2 red (bell) peppers, halved, seeded
      and cut into chunks
    2 orange (bell) peppers, halved,
      seeded and cut into chunks
    2 red onions, each cut into
      6 wedges
    4 garlic cloves
    1 green chilli, seeded and chopped
    30ml/2 tbsp sesame oil
    salt and ground black pepper

1 Trim the alligator steaks so they are similar in size. Put them in a large china or glass dish and add the lime juice, shallot, red chilli, soy sauce and sesame oil. Turn the steaks in the flavouring ingredients and then cover the dish with clear film (plastic wrap). Set the steaks aside in a cool place to marinate while cooking the vegetables.

COOK'S TIP
The flavours in this dish are quite robust, so it is best to serve the steaks and Cajun vegetables with something simple like buttered pasta or rice.

2 Preheat the oven to 230°C/450°F/ Gas 8. Mix the chunks of red and orange peppers, onion wedges, garlic and chilli in a large roasting pan. Add the sesame oil and seasoning and toss well.

3 Roast the vegetables in the preheated oven for about 30 minutes, stirring them occasionally to prevent them from sticking to the pan.

4 Preheat a non-stick griddle pan or frying pan until very hot. Remove the alligator steaks from the marinade using a slotted spoon and cook them in the hot pan for 8–10 minutes on each side, or until cooked through. Brush the steaks with marinade occasionally to keep them moist during cooking. Serve the steaks with the Cajun vegetables, garnished with chopped coriander.

MARINATED WILD BOAR WITH MUSHROOMS

WILD BOAR TASTES LIKE RICH, GAMEY BEEF. HERE IT IS COOKED SLOWLY, WITH LOTS OF SHIITAKE MUSHROOMS AND STOUT, TO MAKE A WONDERFULLY SUCCULENT CASSEROLE.

SERVES FOUR

INGREDIENTS
900g/2lb lean wild boar, trimmed
  and diced
2 large onions, chopped
3 garlic cloves, chopped
900ml/1½ pints/3¾ cups stout
60ml/4 tbsp sunflower oil
450g/1lb/6½ cups shiitake
  mushrooms, halved
15ml/1 tbsp plain (all-purpose) flour
5ml/1 tsp freshly ground
  black pepper
30ml/2 tbsp redcurrant jelly
30ml/2 tbsp chopped fresh parsley
salt

VARIATION
Shiitake mushrooms have a wonderfully strong flavour. If you prefer a milder taste, then use a mixture of chestnut, oyster and button (white) mushrooms.

1 Put the boar in a large, shallow china or glass dish with the onions, garlic and stout. Marinate for at least 2 hours, stirring occasionally. Strain the meat and onions, reserving the stout.

2 Heat the oil in a large, flameproof casserole and fry the meat with the onion and garlic in batches until browned. Set the meat aside. Add the mushrooms a handful at a time, adding more when the previous batch have reduced in volume.

3 Mix the flour with a little of the reserved marinade to make a smooth paste. Return the meat to the casserole and pour in the stout with the flour paste. Mix well and bring the casserole slowly to the boil.

4 Reduce the heat and simmer for 1 hour, stirring occasionally. Add the pepper with salt to taste, the redcurrant jelly and the parsley. Simmer for a further 30 minutes, or until the wild boar is melt-in-the-mouth tender.

SKEWERED WILD BOAR WITH GINGER DIPPING SAUCE

MEAT FROM ITALY, BREAD FROM GREECE AND A DIPPING SAUCE FROM CHINA COME TOGETHER IN THIS DISH THAT IS A GOOD EXAMPLE OF FUSION COOKING, BRINGING TOGETHER THE FLAVOURS AND METHODS OF THREE COUNTRIES.

SERVES FOUR

INGREDIENTS
450g/1lb lean wild boar
15ml/1 tbsp clear honey
50g/2oz/¼ cup butter
15ml/1 tbsp dark soy sauce
For the dip
2.5cm/1in piece fresh
  root ginger, peeled and
  finely chopped
30ml/2 tbsp sesame oil
60ml/4 tbsp hoisin sauce
To serve
pitta breads
shredded Iceberg lettuce

1 Soak four bamboo skewers in warm water for about 30 minutes. (This will help prevent them burning.) Cut the wild boar into small, even-size cubes and thread the cubes on to the skewers. Preheat the grill (broiler) to hot.

2 Melt the honey and butter with the soy sauce in a small pan, and brush liberally over the wild boar. Cook the skewered meat under the grill, for about 12 minutes, turning frequently, and brushing with extra glaze.

3 Meanwhile, cook the ginger in the sesame oil in a small pan for a few minutes. Stir in the hoisin sauce. Remove from the heat.

4 Warm the pitta breads under the grill. Split them, then smear a little of the dip over the inside of each pitta and add some lettuce. Serve with the wild boar skewers and the remaining dip.

KANGAROO WITH TAMARIND CHILLI SAUCE

BUTTERED NOODLES AND A LIGHTLY DRESSED MIXED GREEN LEAF SALAD ARE GOOD ACCOMPANIMENTS FOR RICH, DENSE KANGAROO STEAKS IN A SIMPLE SPICY SAUCE.

SERVES FOUR

INGREDIENTS
    4 kangaroo steaks, each weighing
      about 175g/6oz
    buttered noodles and salad,
      to serve
    parsley, to garnish
For the sauce
    15ml/1 tbsp chilli sauce
    45ml/3 tbsp tamarind paste
    15ml/1 tbsp clear honey
    50g/2oz/¼ cup butter

COOK'S TIP
Tamarind paste is available from South-
east Asian food stores, and you may also
find it in some large supermarkets.

1 Preheat the grill (broiler) to high. To
make the sauce, mix together the chilli
sauce, tamarind paste and clear honey
in a small bowl. Melt the butter in a
small pan over a low heat, then pour
the butter into the bowl and blend
into the sauce until it is smooth.

2 Arrange the kangaroo steaks on a grill
rack and brush the sauce liberally over
them. Grill (broil) the steaks for 3–5
minutes, then turn them and brush with
the remaining sauce. Cook the steaks for
a further 3–5 minutes, then serve with
noodles and salad. Garnish with parsley.

BUFFALO STEAKS WITH HORSERADISH CREAM

THE FLAVOUR OF BUFFALO IS VERY LIKE THAT OF BEEF SO, NOT SURPRISINGLY, IT GOES EXTREMELY WELL WITH HORSERADISH CREAM — ONE OF THE CLASSIC BEEF ACCOMPANIMENTS.

SERVES FOUR

INGREDIENTS

    4 buffalo steaks, each weighing
      about 150g/5oz
    25g/1oz/2 tbsp butter
    15ml/1 tbsp sunflower oil
    salt and ground black pepper
    a few whole chives,
      to garnish
    mixed salad leaves, to serve
For the horseradish cream
    15ml/1 tbsp freshly grated
      horseradish (or to taste)
    115g/4oz/½ cup crème fraîche
    15ml/1 tbsp snipped
      fresh chives

1 Season the steaks on both sides with salt and plenty of ground black pepper. Heat the butter and oil in a large frying pan until sizzling. Add the steaks and cook for 3–4 minutes on each side, turning once.

2 Meanwhile, make the horseradish cream. Mix the horseradish, crème fraîche and snipped chives in a small bowl. Serve the steaks with a dollop of horseradish cream, garnish with chives and serve with a mixed leaf salad.

INDEX

Picture acknowledgements

All photographs are by Craig
Robertson and Janine
Hosegood, except the following:
Anthony Blake Photo Library
p10t John Sims; BBC Natural
History Unit p7tl George
McCarthy; Bruce Coleman
Collection p11b Hans Reinhart,
p34b Robert Maier, p42t
Stephen J Krasemann; Cephas
Picture Library p22b Mick Rock;
Food Features Steve Moss p6
and p30b; Planet Earth Pictures
p7tr Peter Stephenson, p7b
M&C Denis-Huot.